The History and Philosophy of Aikido

YOU WILL NEVER SEE AIKIDO IN THE SAME WAY!

OLIVIER GAURIN

"I don't realy know if I am good-natured or not, but at any rate, Sokaku thought being good-natured was foolish [laughter]."

(Stanley A. Pranin, Aiki News #88
– Interview with Tokimune Takeda – 1991)

The reader is advised that this book is résumé. Even though every attempy has been made to confirm its contents, it cannot hope to be an exhaustive or academic study of the history and philosophy of Aikido. Rather its rôle is only to best help practitioners in their research on these subjects.

TABLE OF CONTENTS

The History of Aikido

PREFACE	4
SOURCES WITH CULTURAL ORIGINS	9
INTRODUCTION TO RESEARCH ON HISTORICAL ORIGINS	18
AIKIDO: RECENT HISTORY	25
THE PREHISTORY OF MARTIAL ARTS	28
THE CHINA-JAPAN TRANSIT	34
INTEGRATION	38
THE GREAT HISTORICAL DIVIDE	45
TOWARDS AIKI-JUJUTSU	54
BUT WHO WAS TAKEDA SOKAKU?	57
THE MEIJI ERA	65
WHAT EXACTLY DID MORIHEI DO?	67
THE BIRTH OF AIKIDO	71
AIBIBUDO, AIKI-JUJUTSU OR AIKIDO?	78
DAITO-RYU AIKI-JUJUTSU	80
FROM AIKI-JUJUTSU TO AIKIDO	84
THE TRUTH WITHIN THE FACTS	86
THE "FOUNDATION" OF CURRENT AIKIDO	94

TOWARDS A "MODERN" AIKIDO, BUT IN SEARCH OF ITSELF !	98
WHY THIS TURNING POINT?	102
AIKIDO FORMATION AND THE NATURE OF AIKI IN DAITO RYU	103
ABSENCE OF COMPETITION	111
AIKIDO: LOGICAL REFERENCES	115
WHERE DOES THE TRUTH OF AIKIDO LIE	117
WHO DID WHAT TO AIKIDO?	121
MORIHEI UESHIBA: THE DANCING MAGICIAN	127
WORLDWIDE DISSEMINATION	130
THE HYPERONYM AIKIDO	134
WHAT KIND OF FUTURE AND FOR WHICH AIKIDO?	138
WHY DOES THE DIVIDE CONTINE ON?	141
AIKI!	144
SO WHAT TO DO? AIKIDO'S FOUR GENERIC LAWS	145
NO PAIN, NO GAIN : REALLY?	152
CONCLUSION	155
BE BRAVE!	156

The Philosophy of Aikido

INTRODUCTION	159
OBJECTIVE VALIDITY OR DELIRIOUS POMPOSITY	161
"ESSENCE", YOU SAID?	162
CONCEPTION/SUBSTANCE	165
ONLY A TOOL, ONLY SOME PRINCIPLES.	166
THE ROLE OF SHOBU-AIKI	168
AIKIDO: A DIFFERENT WAY OF THINKING	171
DIVINE IN THE MAYONNAISE?	174
THE TRUE SELF OR NON-SELF	176
A DIFFICULT INTELLECTUAL DILEMMA	188
WHAT, THERE'S A LINK TO PHILOSOPHY ?	190
DISCOURSE THAT STIMULATES	194
DENSITY OF THOUGHT	197
ANSWERS WITHIN THE WORDS	200
IMMANENCE, A UNIVERSAL PRESENCE	205
WHAT IS THE AIKIDO PACT?	206
THE NOTION OF INTIMA	207
CONCORDANCE	209
THE DIRECTION OF LIFE	214
IN A WORD, THE PHILOSOPHY OF AIKIDO	217
POLITICAL AMNESIA!	218

ALARMING PHILOSOPHICAL PRETENSIONS	224
A TOOL, NEVERTHELESS	227
1942	230
AIKIDO'S GORDIAN KNOT MOMENT	235
CONCLUSION	242
EXTRACT	245
CREDITS	247

—ORIGINAL TEXT IN FRENCH—

My GREAT APPRECIATION

FOR HIS PUNCTILIOUS ASSISTANCE TO THE ENGLISH TRANSLATION TO SIR A.M. WILLIAMSON

O.G.

THE HISTORY OF AIKIDO

PREFACE - Aikido was formed in the twentieth century by the martial arts expert Morihei Ueshiba, and it resulted from his contacts with many eclectic sources, mainly Japanese. Known as Ueshiba Moritaka before the war, he was born in 1883 and, long before he died in 1969, he was known to his students as the revered teacher or, in Japanese, *O Sensei*.

Exceptional encounters made throughout his life with other martial arts experts and remarkable individuals in diverse fields—along with his extraordinary personality, talents and genius for synthesis—enabled him to gradually develop this martial art.

I believe we can say—and I will come back to this again and again—that the historical sources of Aikido as far as the life of its founder is concerned, can be divided into five major periods:

1) The "ancient" period, linked to Emperor Seiwa, Chinese Tao, Japanese tegoi, an ancestor of sumo, and the progressive rise to the throne of the Genji, unrecognized successor princes of the Imperial Family from the eighth until the twelfth century;

2) The medieval or what I call the "In-no-Yo" period, years of construction of Japan from the twelfth century until Western interference in it's affairs and the advent of the Meiji era, following the collapse of the Tokugawa Shogunate and subsequently that of the Aizu clan in 1868;

period of the founder—when he also took the Chinese name Wang-Shou-Kao—and, rather than any tendancy to underestimate it, we can cite this with great respect. Although the precise historical and technical quality of this influence is not exactly known today, sources close to the founder said that, upon his return, his practice had changed. It included elements like the spiral and the circle in his technical work and in his shifts during movements, partially differentiating his style from the original, much more "angular" Daito-ryu style of his master Takeda.

On top of that, there have definitely been periodic Chinese teachings—often unofficial but certainly most profound—that had been an influence on Japanese martial arts over centuries. (E. Amdur* has written most widely on this point.)

* *«1.The Chinese Connection: Searching for the Inner Crouching Tigers and Hidden Dragons. Amdur begins his book by arguing for the existence of a deep Chinese connection with Japanese martial arts. As a very general statement, covering a period lasting several centuries, this is unarguable, but the real issues lie beneath the surface. Since Amdur has already made a rough distinction between external and internal martial arts and indicated that his main interest is in the latter, we can expect that his opening chapter will illuminate the relevance of the Chinese connection with Japanese martial arts for the internal power supposedly latent in the latter. The chapter consists of several short, interconnected essays, each of which will be considered below. (Peter Goldsbury, aikiweb - Transmission / Inheritance / Emulation # 16)*

- The ancient Shinto purification techniques of misogi or "misogi no Gyo". This particular influence stems from meeting Kenzo Futaki, a Doctor of Medicine and one of Morihei Ueshiba's pre-war students. He founded the Misogi

- Those of other schools. Over and above his learning under Sokaku Takeda, *directly or indirectly*, Morihei Ueshiba studied the weapons techniques of Japanese schools such as Tenjin Shin'yo-ryu Jujutsu, Goto-ha Yagyu Shingan-ryu, Aioi ryu jujutsu, Togin-ryu, Okumura Nito-ryu, Takenouchi-ryu, Kito-ryu and Suburi-ryu and Kashima Shinto-ryu as well as Ken-jutsu, certainly, but also Tai-jutsu, Jo, Yari, and so on. We know, for example, that from 1937 Morhei Ueshiba invited three high-level teachers to teach courses from these schools in his own Tokyo Kobukan Dojo. In 1939, it was legally registered as a training school—among other things, this gave it exoneration from tax—and, in 1940, it was declared the Kobukai Foundation, soon to be... Aikikai.

He was also probably close to the Yagyu Shinkage-ryu school (fencing) since we know that at least one of his students, Sensei Kosaburo Gejo, was a great expert there during the twenties and thirties. As was Minoru Hirai, founder of Korindo Aikido, who doubtless introduced the important notion of **Tai-Sabaki** in the "new" Aikido of Ueshiba Morihei after the war. N.B. Korindo Aikido or 光輪洞合気道 is a mixture of jujutsu, fencing and Aikido).

- The definite influence of Chinese martial arts. For example, as far as the contemporary era is concerned, the adoption of certain characteristics of Pa-Koua techniques. This happened during the Manchuria

- Those of Sokaku Takeda (1859-1943), an expert in Daito-ryu Aiki-jujutsu and a figure of prime importance in this context. This martial arts expert was a completely anachronistic character and probably one of the last great samurai of the modern era. Before the Pacific War he taught the foundations and the essence —and I will return to **this** later—of ancient Aiki-jujutsu martial techniques ("The Art of Suppleness of Aiki"), formerly called Daito-ryu (The School of the Great East). All the current Aikido techniques*—along with its spirit and martial character—are drawn from this fundamental Daito-ryu repertoire. Indirectly and historically speaking, reference should also be made here to the Ono-ha Itto-ryu sword school, originally taught with Daito-ryu techniques;

* We're talking about Aikido's Tai-jutsu base here (body-to-body, weaponless, and dagger work (Tanto-Dori 短刀 取)) which very often became Ô Sensei's repertoire, as well as the very clear influence of Nito-ryu principles of Daito-ryu. However, with regard to the exclusive use of weapons—especially Morihei Ueshiba's stick and sabre work—the influences are extensive. In my opinion, they also show other more special syncretisms which greatly blurs the picture. However, when it comes to Aikido's weapons work (Buki-waza 武器 技: jo 杖 and ken 剣), outside the dominant influences of Shikage-ryu (from the years 1926-27) and the Kashima-shinto-ryu (circa 1937), other influences on Ueshiba are incredibly obvious. Namely, those of the rather secretive, esoteric and martial techniques of Kuki-shinden 九 鬼 神殿 and Kuki-shin-ryu 九 鬼神流 of the Kuki family (from 1932-33). This school and family were descendants of the noble fourteenth-century warrior, Yakushimaru Ryushin, about whom I'll talk later on.

3) The period of the Meiji era (1868), Taishô (1912), Shôwa (1926)... until 1942 (the Takeda Sokaku transfer), Morihei Ueshiba, and renown for his quintessential Japanese art;

4) The period from 1942 to 1955 marked by the sudden shift from Aiki-jujutsu to the so-called "modern" Aikido when Kisshomaru Ueshiba gave up his professional activities to devote himself full time to the total reorganization of Aikido;

5) The period from 1955 to the present day: subtle but vehement prohibition of any reinterpretation of past years and—inversely—progressive validation of the technical and philosophical concept of "Aikido meaning Peace and no competition".

However, I would be remiss if I did not make it clear that, equally well, rather than taking a historical view, we can divide these sources and influences into two main categories:

1) Those that are purely technical, in other words, ancestral and martial techniques along with techniques that were either refined or revisited;

2) Those that are purely cultural, in other words, related to religion, science, politics, esotericism, philosophies and arts, and so on.

Accordingly and following this pattern, among the sources and influences that are technical in origin, we can cite the following:

Development Association based on misogi, a traditional purification method for body, mind and spirit that is purely Japanese. This method stems directly from the teachings of the philosopher Bonji Kawatsura (1962-1929), the first to formalize and catalog the ancestral Japanese practices of misogi. It is probably the very same Kenzo Futaki who also taught Morihei Ueshiba Shinto deep-breathing purification techniques (shin-kokyu) as well as tori-fune-kogi-undo and furitama movements, that sprung from this important source of his art. In fact, many are still often practiced today in Japan at the beginning of Aikido classes;

- Buddhist-cum-Shinto "Kotodama" purification techniques inherited from Omoto-kyo, a religion founded by Nao Deguchi in 1892. Kotodama is the doctrine "of the living word" or the belief that mystical powers dwell in words and names (according to Omoto, 1927 pamphlet, Editions Omoto) and Aikido was created according to the principles of kotodama. One of the kotodama practices involves loud intonation of fundamental harmonic sounds of A-E-I-O-U as well as, in Morihei Ueshiba's case, the primary sounds of SU, MU and YU—evoking their mystical powers—as a means of approaching the divine. Often associated in the popular imagery with incantation or prayers, it is, in fact, an attempt to find basic resonance between the material world and the vibrations of the universe. So rather than smiling, it's surely better you practice mantras—seriously and at opportune moments—by the light of the moon, for example—while making **irimi-nage** movements with a partner. In this way, you will begin to understand the importance of this kind of research on fundamental sounds in martial arts or in everyday life!

Medical techniques or body care and maintenance along with various work on the body, for example, the influence of Seitai Shido of Haruchika Noguchi (1911-1976) and post-war influence of masters Tomiki and Okumura, for example. Or, as paradoxical and opposite as it may seem, that of pre-war Japanese military gymnastics.

Finally, as I mentioned previously, the considerable influence of the Kuki family and its Kuki-shinden-ryu 九鬼神殿流 and Kuki-shin-ryu 九鬼神流 from 1932-33. However, for several reasons, this influence is paradoxical. Firstly, because it's rarely mentioned and almost secret which, I think, is a sign of its importance. Now I don't know quite how it happened, but there was split between Aikido and the Kuki family after the death of Morihei. Also, it so happens that this Kuki-shinden-ryu school was introduced into the West, doubtless most incorrectly, within the completely dissimilar technical repertoire of... Nin-jutsu (the "Ninja")! Moreover, the name Kuki-shinden-ryu 九鬼神殿流 which can be read in two ways, changed from "The School of the Nine Divine Spirits (with the reading of the character 鬼 ("ki or kami") as divine spirit) to "The School of the Nine Demons". In this latter interpretation, the character 鬼 read as "Oni" being demon or monster. Rather tricky, right?

- The polymath biologist and ecologist Kumagusu Minakata (1867-1941) who introduced him to a humane and ecosystemic, unitary and universalist perception of the world. The concept of interdependent ecosystems forming the unity of the natural world was developed very early by Kumagusu Minakata. In fact, he was one of the first people in the world to define the biological world as an ecosystem—in other words, a systemic structural whole of which each "part" would be in permanent interrelation with all other parts. This is very much in sync with the vision that the founder of Aikido had of the world around him;

* *Ecosystem:* "*This new perspective introduced by contemporary science, reveals the idea of an interdependence of phenomena. So the ecosystem is conceived according to the microbiologist Kumagusu Minakata as "a structural whole in which the soil, water and various plant and animal species, including humans, live in a state of mutual interdependence and evolve in a continuous process of transformation and circulation. As we can see, the shift is fundamental. Going from a vision that privileges separation and opposition to a vision that integrates the human being in a world is a radical upheaval whose ethical consequences can be considerable*" (Linda Stevens).

- The mystical, peaceful and universalist principles of the Japanese Omoto-kyo sect, a branch of animist Shintoism that was paradoxically ultra-nationalistic. This reflected the times and the years described as "The Descent into the Kurai-Tanima (Dark Valley) of Militarism" from 1930 to 1945. These principles were also very closely linked to Japanese right-wing extremists circles of the pre-war period, for example, the relationship between the Kodo-Omoto group

Finally, it should also be understood that the deep ties between Morihei Ueshiba and the Kuki family were reflected during the war by his decision to name Kuki Takaharu—the soke (宗家), main heir) of Kokishinden-ryu—as shinto priest responsible for the famous Iwama Aiki-jinja shrine. And on this occasion, Kuki Takaharu officially offered and officially shared two of his family's Ho 宝 (sacred treasures) with the Iwama sanctuary.

This information is based on research and abstracts by Eric Grousilliat, published in his book: "At the crossroads" (Les Éditions du Net, 2018). Also mainly from the book "Study of Kuki Family Archives" [九鬼文書の研究] by Miura Ichiro (published in 1941). There are also some old books here in Japan on the subject but, since they are above all in Japanese and not focussed on the Kuki family-Morihei Ueshiba relationship, any study of this subject is difficult.

As you will probably have guessed, I could equally well have placed the Kuki family sources among those with cultural origins. In any event, having included them in those with technical origins, we can now safely proceed to take a more detailed look at those with cultural origins.

SOURCES WITH CULTURAL ORIGINS - The sources and individuals that shaped the personality and thinking of Morihei Ueshiba are many and varied, but they include the following that I believe are the most important:

noted—and it's most important to understand this quite incredible link—that this spirituality is, by its Senpo 戦法 or "method of war" (strategy), **a profound joining of Taoism with Shinto**. Here, doubtless like O Sensei at that time, we discover with a feeling of profound deference, the seventh-century origins of Aiki.

Thirdly and finally, the Kuki family influence is paradoxical since the Kuki-shinden-ryu influence is very technical, especially with regard to O Sensei's weapon techniques at Iwama. Indeed, this technical side of Kuki-shinden-ryu provided many bases or forms—even "prototypes"—of the Buki-waza kata that could later be observed in Morihei Ueshiba's work. And thus modern Aikido's weapons work as I've already mentioned.

Moreover—and certainly not the least important "historic detail"—it's paradoxical because this cross-breeding, this intimate, technical and spiritual relationship Ueshiba had with Kuki-shinden-ryu, also gave rise to the birth of the notion of **Takemusu-aiki** (武産合気). A notion which is often raised when discussing the breakaway of modern Aikido. In fact, Takemusu Aikido is the "Ame-no-mura-kumo-samuhara-Aikido" [天之村雲九頭龍武産合気道] which, I believe, can be translated as "the Aikido of the ancient times of villages under the charm of the drizzly clouds". A term which comes from the Dragon-king god 龍王 of the same name as "the dragon king of ancient time... and so on". Is it finally starting to make some sense?

18

The second reason the Kuki family influence is paradoxical is, in fact, polyvalent in nature. Firstly, it's historically prestigious in that their knowledge came directly from the fourteenth-century chivalrous epic of their forebear Ryushi Yakushimari, one of the great heroes of the Fujiwara clan. He rescued and liberated His Imperial Majesty Emperor Godaigo—Southern Court—whose historical legitimacy was only recognized in 1911, from the clutches of Ashikaga Takauji, future shogun and main supporter of "The Northern Imperial Court" of Emperor Komyo. This occured during the sixty-year war Nanboku-cho (南北朝 時代) between the North and South Imperial Courts. Emperor Godaigo thanked Ryushi for his rescue by bestowing on him the family name "Kuki 九鬼", which means "nine divine spirits (九)" as opposed to nine demons". Even if we ignore the esoteric meaning of the number nine—in the Tao, it's the "angular" figure representing the incessant, sinusoidal tilting of In and Yo—it was also an allusion to Ryushi's stick technique, namely to his *naginata* shaft whose blade had broken in the fight. In front of the Emperor, Ryushi had even named his technique "Kuji" (九字)"or "the technique of nine letters".

Secondly, the family influence is esoteric : Rejutsu 霊術 and Kukireijutsu 九鬼霊術, that is to say, "The Shinto Spirituality of the Kuki". Since this was consistent with Morihei's research, we finally see a coherent and historically legitimate cross between martiality and spirituality. For Morihei Ueshiba, it was the authentic Tenshin-hyoho 天眞兵, namely "The warrior rules of the truth of the sky". It should be (previous name of Omoto-kyo) and the pro-fascist and xenophobic party Dai Nippon Seisanto*.

Of particular note in this regard, is the privileged mystical relationship Morihei Ueshiba maintained with Onisaburo Deguchi (1871-1948), one of the two leaders of the Omoto religious movement. It is known that Morihei Ueshiba heard about the Omoto sect around 1912, became a member in 1920, and taught his Aiki-jujutsu to sect members at Ayabe, near Kyoto. This exceptional encounter brought to his art a characteristically Shinto spiritual approach and a high-level "cosmic" character—paradoxically also related to the social policy of his time and to the inner secrets of the Japanese political power. The political fringes of the Omoto-kyo sect later turned on Morihei Ueshiba, and he only owed his salvation to his high-level political connections, including those with the War Ministry.

On this subject, see Deguchi Onisaburo, the "October incident" and Omoto-Kyo's relations with part of the Japanese ultra-nationalist right at the time (Morihei Ueshiba was then head of Dai Nippon Senyokaï (association for the promotion of the Budo, branch of Showa Seinenkai (youth organization of Showa, "rather" revolutionary" para-military force, it was in 1931), and if the site is still online, extracts from the thesis from Nadolski, by P. Goldsbury on: http//www.aikiweb.com/

- The indirect influence of traditional Japanese martial arts body building work of Jigoro Kano, founder of judo. Morihei Ueshiba wanted to copy his popularized teaching system—apparently successful and thriving—but, in this case, to use it to transform elitist Aiki-jujutsu techniques of self defense into "educational techniques for all". N.B. Morihei Ueshiba had studied judo in his youth in Tanabe around 1911, and remained in close contact with the judo founder throughout his life.

- The definite influence at the political and social level: this was, in fact, an out-and-out "bath" or environment in which O Sensei himself evolved. The political and social environment of pre-war Japanese militarism from the 1920s to roughly 1942, was in retrospect not particularly glorious. Nor, for example, were the "Cherry Blossom Society" (Sakurakai) and other militaristic, ultra-nationalist associations and factions which, thanks to his associates or choice of teachers, he mixed with. "What I want to say here is that while Morihei Ueshiba was a very patriotic Japanese, he was considerably to the right of the political spectrum." (*Peter Goldsbury, Aikiweb, #7 Transmission - Inheritance - Emutaltion*).

His long post-war retreat in Iwama up until the 1950s is directly linked to his past, and—due to political involvement stemming from his former activities with the ultra military—there is a real "Gordion Knot" moment to Aikido. I will talk about it again since this is what binds the history of Aikido with its philosophy. For example, "Not many people know that in early spring of the fifth year of the Showa era (1930), Ueshiba participated in contests (organized inter-disciplinary duels) at the Japanese Imperial Academy." (*Article by Christopher Li: "The Spiritual Leap— Moritaki (Morihei) Ueshiba in 1932" on the very informative website of Aikido Sangenkai in Hawai*).

- Finally there is another cultural influence—ancestral and Japanese par excellence—namely that of the "magical" rural quality or countryside feeling of the lands, forests and mountains of Japan. "Morihei Ueshiba was born in Tanabe, a sleepy country town located on the coast of the Kii peninsula. Just behind the town lies a vast mountain range, which was at the end of an ancient Kyoto pilgrimage route dating back at least to the Heian period. There were two popular devotional centres here, each with a long history: Kumano Sanzan shrines (Shinto) and Koya-san, the centre of Shingon Buddhism. Given the exploits of Ueshiba after his return from military service in 1907, it is highly likely that not only did the inhabitants of the city think he had learned his martial skills from the mythical Tengu mountain creatures, but also that Ueshiba himself believed it". (*Aikiweb, Peter Goldsbury, #7, note n°8 Transmission - Inheritance - Emulation*).

And so we see that it was these diverse influences which, among other things, shaped the personality and thinking of Morihei Ueshiba. And it was this ensemble that actually formed the "material" for the construction of his art of Aikido.

Then, especially after the Pacific War, he himself partially transformed or pruned his master Sokaku Takeda's original martial techniques. And he did this based on his own actual personal experience: cultural, martial, mystical, vital, political, diverse, social and intense as it was. We also know today that he didn't often divulge his sources or his "tricks"—a ruse which, until the end of his days, often allowed him to leave spectators of his work astounded by his prowess. Moreover, by the end of his lifetime, the Morihei Ueshiba "technique" was completely integrated with his mystical thinking about the universe. So much so in fact, that very few of his students could even begin to approach the depth of his teaching which too often waxed lyrical with rather obscure vocabulary.

In the wake of his death in 1969—and in the void it left behind—his descendants, as well as the majority of his former students, decided to categorically standardize Aikido based on pragmatic, pedagogical and popular criteria.

Other students went in different teaching directions and separated from the Ueshiba family branch (Aikikai of Tokyo) to create personal or fusion branches of Aikido. However, they were "strongly" urged to change the name of their teaching—something that is done and was commonly done in Japan, for example, in the Ko-ryu pre-Meiji-era schools.

INTRODUCTION TO RESEARCH ON HISTORICAL ORIGINS

 - The reader should be warned that any attempts at historical research on the subject of Aikido will inevitably come up against many obstacles. There is, above all, a lack of historical documents—or serious difficulty in accessing them—as well as a scattering of historical references. To this we must add confused or directed testimony, a Japanese culture notoriously complex to decipher, a language no less difficult if not completely closed to the layman, difficulties in certifying facts or testimonies, great silences, words that cannot be spoken, taboos, and so on. However, as far as is possible, I wanted here to reframe the history of Aikido within the perspective of a much wider historical context than is usual.

The official story limits the genealogy of Aikido to the twentieth-century period and, in fact, to the life of Morihei Ueshiba—an approach which I think neither very logical nor very enterprising. This is especially true if we also know his successors voluntarily abandoned the core values that Aikido's founder prioritized in the development of his art. If we also know that he himself too often eluded—dodged explaining you might say—the grounds as well as the ins and outs and results of his own experimentation. This is also true of his own teaching in which he voluntarily—or at least consciously—limited passing on all that he knew and all that he did.

In this way, many points remain open to question in the work of historical reconstruction whereby I will make a more serious attempt to look behind the convenient "screen" masking the life of O Sensei, usually told in stereotypes or idealized images. In this effort, rather than simply trotting out a series of convictions, I am going to attempt to test them by trying to gather and cross-reference information currently available into a final, coherent panorama—even if the information will not always be fully "certified".

Thank you for your understanding, your intelligence and your willingness to understand these "blurs" or lack of precision inherent in the "summary" nature imposed by the framework of this attempt. Having said that, I think it's time we really got to grips with the research.

AIKIDO: RECENT HISTORY

Aikido is originally what was called after the war a **Shin-Budo** (new martial art) or what is called a **Gendai Budo** in Japan today. That is to say it is a post-Meiji-era, contemporary martial art that is unlike the **Ko-ryu** (**Ko-budo**) or **Koden** "old schools" existing or founded between 1192 and 1868. The art of Aikido was, in fact, founded and fixed in its main principles of "**Do**" in Japan by the martial arts expert Morihei Ueshiba (1883-1969)—He also went under the first names Tsunemori, Seigan, and Moritaka during his life—and his work took place during the preceeding century, in the years following the 1942-1945 war in the Pacific.

Following his death in 1969, his son Kisshomaru—as well as many of his direct or indirect pupils—were absolutely intent on effectively synthesizing his work.* It was already defined by the term "Aikido", but they wanted to "transplant" it beyond its historical roots, and their intent was fiercely buttressed by a foundation built on three fundamental criteria:

- A modern and innovative character—the antithesis of traditionalism;

- A popularized pedagogy (*vox populis rex*) of "the good";

- An international development perspective.

* *Reflection of Kisshomaru Ueshiba, when Japan had just lost the war and capitulated: " The exercise of military power based on militarism and nationalism has been shown to be a mistake, as is evidenced by our present situation. Certainly there is much of Japanese culture that we can be proud of, but now the war has ended, the evaluation of this has fallen to zero. Just the same, there is one part of this culture to which I myself am directly connected: Aikido that my own father created. Even though I have not progressed so far in Aikido, I believed that Aikido was an excellent part of this culture: not merely the waza, but especially the spiritual aspects of this budo. I wanted some day to take Aikido to America and Europe and say, "Look! There is something good here, even from Japan. It is a budo without fighting and with a positive philosophy towards the opponent. If you are interested, I will teach you. If not, please teach me what you have that is good. I thought that defeated Japan had something precious to offer the nations that had won the war and that emphasizing what was valuable would help to achieve Japan's reconstruction and rebirth. Especially now, in the present circumstances, Aikido has a role to play in Japan's reconstruction. In fact, it is because of its spiritual aspects that Aikido should play such a role.. " (This is what Kisshomaru Ueshiba wrote in his first manifesto for Aikido.) He was 25. And all his life he worked in this direction (Aikikai Foundation, "Aikido Ichiro," pp. 22-23).*

Within the framework of this presentation and a few lines further on, we will return to this contemporary aspect of this twentieth-century martial art. But right now, let's take a big step back in time, far, far away from the adventures of this "modern" founder. For this masterpiece of Morihei Ueshiba that we call "Aikido" already has within itself a binary descent: a historical and a geographical one.

Aikido doesn't emerge out of "nowhere"—a sort of historical vacuum*—or only from the martial genius of its "composer". In reality, this art has its origins in much older, very precise, codified technical sources. Of course, while these sources are sometimes a little blurred by their overlapping, they are sometimes correctly indexed, as is strikingly exemplified by Ueshiba's epic 1933 technique compilation *Budo Renshu*.

* "People in this world look at things mistakenly, and think that what they do not understand must be some kind of vacuum or emptiness. But it's not a vacuum. It's just bewilderment." (Christopher Li – Aikido Sangenkai:" A Leap of the Spirit – Moritaka (Morihei) Ueshiba in 1932")

So now it's appropriate to take a journey back in time and take a closer look at some of those older sources. In fact, we shall have to go as far as the pre-history of martial arts.

THE PREHISTORY OF MARTIAL ARTS

- For readers who have not read the presentation on this period in my book *My Aikido Memento* (in French), I would like to recapitulate the broad outlines of this ancient period below.

It would be incorrect to assume that martial arts—and here I mean the art of overcoming—were not enacted in "schools" (in the broad sense of the word) or more or less codified, most often secretly, very early in the history of mankind. From the moment combat groups, bands or even armies, put in place more or less standardised hierarchical strategies and tactics, means of organized combat—however rudimentary—or shared arms, it is almost certain these advances were also developing at another level. And here I mean shared technical knowledge of combat as well as coordination and learning synergies which gave a community, an individual or even a party a greater chance of winning. Certainly such developments were taking place in the art of hunting and its secrets—no doubt in concert.

Yet, surprisingly, when it comes to martial arts "schools" or "movements" in general, though some historians speak of 5,000 years, it's be difficult to go back much further than a few millennia before Jesus Christ. One must be circumspect on this issue since—quite quickly—one reaches the point where there are few reliable archaeological traces. From what we know today, as far as Europe is concerned, I would point out that the first quite reliable archaeological traces of some codified martial styles reveal that it was Mediterranean and Mesopotamian centres* that came to improve or strongly influence a broad intercontinental martial arts current—interchange or colonistic in nature—towards the East as far as the Himalayan foothills (North India, China, Tibet ...). This influence did not happen quickly, but rather over hundreds or even thousands of years and, as we will see shortly, had its effect on Japan in those remote times.

* *As far back as ancient Greece, of course, since the first traces of a Greek civilization go back to what is called its "archaic era" in the 8th/6th century BC; or further south in Egypt where the first royal period (first dynasty around 2900 BC) marked the birth of three millennia of Pharaonic events.*

Other accepted sources of very ancient combat arts and sciences established in "schools", existed also in the south of the continent, for example, in Southern India. Historical sources, however, suggest there were no deep external continental influences there, and this leads one to think there was a greater "autonomy" of thinking and development in this area. These other far distant sources of Aikido are to be found then in South-East India (Tamil country) and, interestingly for us here, more precisely on the Malabar coast.

"The Malabar Coast—and yes, it's true that the word *malabar* comes to us from there—stretching from upper Kerala to Cape Comorin, the tip of the subcontinent, has always been separated from the rest of India by the Western Ghats mountain range. This explains why the inhabitants of Malabar had their very earliest contact with seafaring peoples: traces of Phoenician colonies have been found; teak pillars from India were found in Mesopotamia; the Jews of King Solomon knew the inhabitants of Malabar since the Tamil word *tokai* (peacock) became *tuki* in Hebrew. In addition, many Roman and Greek travelers, such as Pliny the Elder, have left very precise descriptions of the Malabar coast, and so it can be said that Vasco de Gama only "rediscovered" a territory the ancient world had already known for a long time".*

* Extract from an article published in "Jaïa Bharati", by François Gautier, who is also the author of the remarkable book "Another Look on India" (in French), Tricorne, 2001.

On the Malabar Coast then, "martial arts schools" with very secret techniques—and similarly reserved teaching approaches—were, in large part, the source of the truly amazing martial arts of Kalaripayat (literally "the place of exchange of the exercises", doubtless dating back to around 3000 BCE) as well as Varma Kalai, "The Art of Vital Points" dating back with certainty to around 2500 BCE.

While oral history has it that the Indian art of Kalaripayat was itself transmitted from India to China in the sixth century, partisans of today's omnipotent China naturally believe the reverse to be true! The fact is that the vector of this transmission was the Indian Buddhist monk Da Mo Sardili or Bodhidarma—"Bodai Daruma" in Sanscript—who taught the monks of the Shaolin Chinese temple. In fact, the very famous Japanese "Daruma" traditional doll is modelled after him. For the record, it was also Da Mo Sardili who introduced China to the famous Buddhist doctrine named "Chan" (called "Dhyana" in India) which is now better known as "Zen Buddhism". And it is there we find, in an interesting interlinkage with Japanese religious syncretism, the reason why Buddhist doctrines and Aikido still sometimes overlap. For example, the expression "polish the mirror"—so dear to the late Osawa Kisaburo Sensei (1911-1991), the father of Master Osawa Hayato (1951-)—comes from these Buddhist principles*.

* *Zen Buddhism and Aikido: Ther are reports of "collusion and ideological fraternity"—as as well as practices that may be deemed old—between Aikido and Zen Buddhism. However, although many of the highly ranked or highly recognized Aikido sensei advocate Zen in the practice of Aikido—and for an important reason I'll bring up next—in my opinion, it is mostly a question of Zen's meddling and inegalitarian political links with Aikido. In fact, the main root of Aikido is not in Buddhism or the Zen of "Bodai Daruma", but in the philosophical Tao (so non-religious) and even more so in Shinto, with neither Tao nor Shinto being Buddhistic. And this makes a huge difference. However,* *typical Japanese syncretism leads to these three--"Shinto-Buddhism-Tao"--very often being put on the same plane or in "the same bag". Obviously this phenomenon occurs similarly in the West, with the exaggeration that can only be guessed, genre "the Master points at the moon, and the student gazes at at his finger".*

*But care must be exercised here since there are also parallels to be made between these three and Confucianism, a secular, on-religious philosophy, as I recall. Yet curiously, when discussing Aikido, we never talk about Confucianism. It would be very interesting to ask, "Why do we talk so much about Zen, and so little about Confucianism?" The answer is that Zen has many facets. Firstly, it pays great respect to notions that are finally "acceptable" about our fate, for example, in old days, samurais' acceptance of the idea of sacrifice or death. In other words, it was a question of the lower ranks developing the capacity to obey, in an acceptable and dignified way, the laws—divine, of course—at the discretion of the "powerful elite". The second most important aspect of Zen is what I call "the Shaolin facet". Indeed the idea of "Bodaï Daruma" in Shaolin was twofold: on one hand, to bring the truth of that religion to the monks; but on the other, to strengthen them in their bodies. Here we once again find the very classical Japanese notion of Bunburyodo (文武両道) the common way of knowledge and military arts, which was, and still is, the great ideal of Japanese warrior in the Land of the Rising Sun. And, like the samurai throughout history, it is in this return to time of Zen body strengthening that Aikido sensei drew their fascination for the Chan religion. Indeed, over and above the religious aspect itself, Zen is also a school of **Ki**, power.*

*The best example of this kind of research in Aikido is, of course, Tohei Sensei with his passion for "**Ki**", and his "performances" which can still appear surprising and mysterious today. Because, how did he fortify this Ki? By practicing Zen and therefore Zazen meditation to excess! Although I personally do not like the term, we find here what is called in the West the "internal channels" of the martial arts. This is not a question of a search for some kinds of superpowers, but only of how to generate increased power, additional power that is viewed by the layman as verging on the supernatural. And this, without going through the purely muscular system of the body, in other words, tendon strengthening, release of internal energy flows, use of facias, kokyu-ryoku, power transmissions, mental-body unity, enhanced health, and so on. This is a concentration of reactualized breathing, of relaxation, and of channeling, extension and concentration of energies inside our own body.*

*However, make no mistake about it: Zen provides fabulous keys to these kinds of discovery and development in Aikido. And also, for example, Russian sytema which is probably the martial art most similar to the original Aiki, without all the hotchpotch of "mysticology" that Morihei Ueshiba's Aikido developed. Systema, which has nothing religious about it, allows the same energy concentration as well, if not better, through exercises using the same principles or channels of internal body powers. So we can say that the facet of Zen is therefore double-acting and double-edged: ideological, moral and religious cutting edge **and** the cutting edge of "internal" bodily strengthening. And at this point, yes, we can begin to ask ourselves if Aikido is actually the indirect support for this internal work (its "shell") or if this internal work is the effective and direct governor of Aikido. But here I choose to leave the question unanswered.*

*Confucianism, on the contrary, provides inestimable services to these same "power people", the political elite because it makes it possible for them to "manage" the lower orders. It's just a matter of the chiefs, the masters correctly developing the faculties and knowledge intended for command. Confucianism and Zen are therefore not only interrelated, but also very closely linked to historic Japanese social and political ideology. Both are therefore very useful for the elite of the system or teachers to put into place in Aikido as well. However, this implementation is done at two speeds—secretly for Confucianism and openly for Zen—because both Zen and Confucianism—once assembled adroitly—allow for better control of lower orders-customers-practitioners. But here, Confucius equals secret! So we don't talk about it, and it is not included in study for "lambda" practitioners. But, at the upper levels of Japanese society, everything is organized according to Confucian principles, namely vertical hierarchy, command/order systems, formation of groups, personal relationships between Masters and disciples, ideologies of power, and types of education. In other words, pedagogy, absence of contradiction, and so on. While Zen is put forward for all, it will make practitioners much more zealous, docile and servile. Here, Zen means popularization: "Practice Zen, children. Zen is good for mental and physical health—"for sure, it's quiet—and for morale—"Uh... excuse me, Master, but is not it rather for **the** morality?" And so practice this wonderful Zazen with the help of salutary sticks, along with the cleaning and polishing of your souls and floors so that they shine like the calm pond at dawn. Besides, Zen is like altogether like Aikido. After all, is it just a coincidence that, for decades during the post-war period, we've said that Aikido is Zen in motion?" My goodness, what a fabulous proof of the ideological whole of these good words! What divine reasoning! What could be better for the world than Aikido?*

*If one wants to talk about the "Zen and Aikido" theme, I don't really mind at all. In fact, it's perhaps a good idea. But then, along with Japanese Buddhism, to preserve our integrity, we're going to have to talk about Japanese Confucianism, the Japanese Tao, and Japanese Shinto. And along with them, the influence of the Omoto religion, still very much present in the upper background of today's Aikido. Finally, we have to talk about **Ki** and that, my friend, is the big thorny question here. But why don't you ask the Russian systema people to explain a little to you. Because, in terms of Aikido, these five philosophies have—or had—their influences, but not at all for the same reasons, and not at all for the same "customers", and not at all for the same purpose!*

As a reminder, I would point out that, by his motto "Martial practice is a body prayer" as well as his knowledge and exceptional personality, Da Mo Sardili profoundly transformed both the religious and martial vision of these Shaolin warrior monks. And this, at a time when they—interestingly for us here—were already standing at the geographical "hub" of two great martial arts movements: Northern China techniques (distant combat: long-legs techniques) and those of Southern China (close combat: short-hand techniques). Da Mo Sardili brought to these established Chinese movements not only "his" art—or certainly many of the secret facets of Kalaripayat—but also, as we have seen, depth and spiritual vision. And, it is of particular note that Da Mo Sardili brought a surprising physiological depth to the art, this time oriented towards the health and internal power of combatants.

We next move towards the year one thousand—several centuries later if one takes any pleasure in following the arrow of time. And it was at that juncture—most likely mainly from deep China with its Qinna or Chin-Na techniques of "dislocations and gripping"—that the Japanese technical roots of hand-to-hand combat were extrapolated or perfected. Later in the Islands of the Rising Sun, they were to be called "Aiki-jujutsu", a term which literally means:

- Technique: **Jutsu** or "Jitsu";
- Soft: **Jû** or **Ju** ("Yawarakai" or in Japanese, "the soft way"). And that's the most difficult both to understand and to put into practice;
- Energy: **Ki**;
- Completive concordance "in the heart of ": **Ai***.

*It should be pointed out that the notion of "completive concordance" lies at the heart of the problem of understanding Aikido. It basically means the mental conditions which—even if one isn't aware of it—complement one another or get in tune together like an orchestra before a concert. And this, within the context of an aggression, confrontation or attack—or even an opponent's mental intention or move to initiate such a situation.

In any event, before we address this complex issue in further detail, there is another important question that almost immediately comes to mind.

THE CHINA-JAPAN TRANSIT - The question arises of just how this transit came about, and, in addressing it, we can't ignore the obvious possibility of transmission of ancient Chinese martial knowledge via the Okinawa Islands (former Kingdom of Ryukyu), in direct transit towards the Japanese archipelago. However, as far as the Aiki routes are concerned, it appears clear today that transmission did not pass through Okinawa at all.

We cannot overemphasize this fact because an Okinawa transit would have been much more direct. Indeed, this route was closely linked to the cultural orientations of the Japanese ruling court of **Emperor Seiwa*** (56th of the line: 850-880).

> * "I would like to begin by asking you some questions about your father, Sokaku Takeda. Can it be said that he created the art of Daito-ryu?
> Tokimune Takeda: "No, the art's origins lie in an art called "tegoi". There is a story about this art in the Kojiki, the book of ancient Japanese history and mythology. When the goddess Amaterasu Omikami went to her fellow god Takeminakata no Mikoto to order him to return her country to her, he and the god Takemikazuchi no Mikoto fought a memorable match. This match was conducted using tegoi, which can be considered to be the origin of present-day sumo. In ancient times, sumo matches were held at shrine festivals. Emperor Seiwa created the two Imperial Guard corps of Ukon and Sakon, and made sumo into a martial art. Later, during the Kamakura period, sumo became the most popular martial art. Therefore, it can be said that Emperor Seiwa is the founder of Daito-ryu. ....The record of this story is kept at the Grand Ise Shrine and, although these documents are not shown to anyone except Shinto priests, I was permitted to see them since the Takeda family is descended from a family of priests. When I went there to check out what my father had told me, I found these documents." (Interview with Tokimune Takeda, son of Takeda Sokaku (Stanley A. Pranin, AikiNews #87)

In fact, by the 9th century AD, some 16,000 Chinese scrolls or manuscripts had already been deciphered and scrupulously studied in Japan (source: Nihon-koku genzaisho-mokuroku). It is through the Oe family of Japanese scholars, high dignitaries of the Japanese court and Chinese literature specialists—inter alia **Oe no Koretoki** (10th century), author of several martial arts anthologies—that this specific knowledge was introduced and archived directly in the Japanese kingdom's Imperial Court.

Later, his successor **Oe no Masafusa***, who bore the title "Temporary Intermediate Counselor of the Emperor" and was a noted specialist in Chinese

Taoism, continued his work. We also know from reliable sources that the Chinese dualistic philosophy of Yin and Yang ("**On'yo-Do**" in Japanese: 陰陽道)— or On'yo-Do, Onmyo-Do, and also In'yo-Do— actually flourished very early in Japan—during the 9th century, in fact. When we understand that the duties of court functionaries of the time—and equally important the secrets of their exploitation—were very fiercely defended and transmitted from generation to generation, we can better understand the historical continuation of the development of these Chinese sources.

* *Oe no Masafusa (1041-1111), Imperial Councilor, was a famous scholar and Japanese tutor under emperors Shirakawa, Horikawa and Toba. Oe no Masafusa has become especially famous in Japan for being the author of "The Book of Annual Celebrations" by Goke Shidaï.*

Another source directly cites one of Emperor Seiwa's sons—he had nineteen children—as co-inventor or discoverer of "Aiki-jujutsu" at the same time and also from Chinese sources. In addition to combined knowledge of Tao and Chinese martial arts—even if I don't know the historical name of that era's Chinese Chin-Na techniques—in view of common techniques, it is clear that the transmission link is absolutely direct. But I must admit I couldn't glean a lot of information on this subject. It would be the sixth son of Emperor Seiwa, Prince Teijun, who—among others—would transmit the Aiki principles to the generations that followed, including through his own son, Tsunemoto Minamoto (894-961). At this point, Aiki was technically linked to the ancient forms of indigenous sumo reserved for samurai castes, a traditional sumo called tegoi. The foundational Japanese Shinto text, Kojiki, contains literary references to this form of struggle, describing the combat of the god Takeminakata with the god Takemikazuchi*. And it is probably for this reason that there has always been a very great complicity between sumo and Aiki techniques—even up to very recent times. It is even sometimes said that tegoi itself was transmitted under the name of "Aiki In no Yo no Ho" ("the method of Yin and Yang of Aiki"), and this right up to the Kamakura period (1192-1333).

* *"... When the god Takeminakata seized the hand of the god Takemikazuchi, his hand became like a pillar of ice, and on the opposite side, the other hand of the god Takemikazuchi changed into a sword blade. In this way, the god Takeminakata lost all hope of winning. Then in turn the god Takemikazuchi seized the hand of the god Takeminakata, held it as if it were just a young reed and threw it away.*

But later, in the same continuous Imperial line of ancient Japan—closely related to Taoism and Chinese culture—we move forward two centuries to the years of government of the Japanese regents of the eleventh century. These two centuries precede the rise to power of the Genji*, a lineages of princes who progressively became warriors. Their gradual rise would finally result in the brilliant establishment of the **Genji**-Minamoto clan through the so-called "Genpei" war 源平合戦. This epic of this long war—five years—inspired the famous historical novel *The Heike's Tale* 平家物語). This conflict between the Taira clan and the Minamoto threw Japan of the time into some twenty terrible battles, from the north (Honshu) to the south and almost as far as Kyushu. And it was the last battle, the great naval battle of Dan-no-ura in the Shimonoseki Strait, which was decisive for the Minamoto. The advent of the Minamoto who annihilated the Taira and went on to establish their capital at Kamakura, would mark the end of the era of Heian nobles' power. However, everything is relative since the Fujiwara, for example, continued to exercise positions of Japanese political power. And this, up until the twentieth century and the beginning of what will be called "The Kamakura period", by the 1192 establishment of the famous "Bakufu 幕府 of Kamakura", or the first Shogunal Government!

** The word **"Genji"** (Heian period (794-1185), is the ancient Chinese reading of "Minamoto" (Japanese reading).The **"Genji"** were surnames attributed by the emperors of that time, officially certifying the lineage of princes removed from Imperial succession (the "Genji", or Radiant Prince of the famous Tale of Genji ("Genji-Monogatari") was thus a son of the Emperor Kiritsubo, who could not claim the throne). So it is that we say "the Genji" although this name also became a proper name, in this case that of ... of ...? Yes, good answer: That of ... Minamoto!*

And so it was that, here in the Islands of the Rising Sun, this foundation or base—already very well developed at the technical level—would not only be transformed and crossed with, but also perfected through the use of local weapons and warfare skills necessitated by the incessant struggles raging between the many factions or fiefdoms. And we shall soon see how the very nature of Japanese weaponry had an important influence on the integration of these Chinese martial arts techniques.

INTEGRATION - It is indisputable that the Japanese sword—not only quite different from Chinese weapons in its form, but also in its qualities, its wearing and especially its use, as well as the attitudes and body protocols it imposes—had an influence on the indigenous adaptation and shaping of technical martial arts discourse from China. And that influence—while both decisive and foundational—was finally ostracized*. To this, we can add its corollary—the making and wearing of dedicated armor—as well as that of the continual experimentation in one-on-one or group combat on battlefields in older times, for example, in Japan of the bushi or samurai.

*Quintessential Japanese-style technical appropriation follows a typical pattern: (1) careful study of a particular subject; (2) copying or, where possible, adoption; (3) development in accordance with local factors; (4) disconnection and possession or "we can do better" (5) typical Japanese reconstruction—both factual and environmental; (6) untimately conceptual independence; (7) a sense of originality considered, rightly or wrongly, to be both superior and exportable; (8) rejection of the subject's origins.
This last step is also a feature of the development of Aikido, and, up until today, there has been a rejection of its Chinese origins. And, as is usual with the phenomenon of ostracism, the corollary or an implacable

defiance manifesting itself, in this case, by the Aikikai assertion, "It's Morihei who invented Aikido!". Why not, indeed, since there are good reasons for this.

Thanks to the rise in power of this warrior class within the Japanese political power structure of the time, martial arts specializations took shape and, by necessity, gradually became integrated at a high level to become truly and culturally Japanese.

Over time then, as a result of practical study, Japanese integration of continental fighting techniques gave rise to what was called, among other things, the art of In-Yo-Ho (or In-no-yo-no-Ho), which literally means "The Law of Use of Yin and Yang Synergy". I think this can be translated intellectually by the expression below—an expression which, for us Cartesians believing mind and body to be separate, is difficult to understand.

"THE WAY OF FORCE
LESS THE WAY OF WEAKNESS
MUST BE EQUAL TO ZERO"

In other words, to survive, you must work to end up with a "zero force" result.*

Read also my first work Understanding Aikido (French) —page 124 in the first edition, page 88 in the second edition, at Budo Editions, France—for details and justification of this interpretation.

* *"Zero"—the void, emptiness, vacuum—which is also in several* *languages of the world at the origin of the words "digit", "coding", and "ciphering", all forms of encoding. Zero is designated in most languages by a circle, an oval or a big dot, symbolizing the **celestial vault** and therefore the void or nothing, hence the term comes from the Arabic word sifr, literally meaning empty or nothing.*

The art of In-Yo-Ho was, in fact, cited for the first time in the Japanese martial arts treatise *Bugei-Shoden*, around the year one thousand. This art—mainly related to **Taoism** of Chinese origin—underwent constant improvement in the utmost secrecy over several generations within the family of the famous samurai and ruling clan leader, **Shinra Saburo Minamoto** or **Genji no Yoshimitsu** (circa 1045-1127), 6th direct descendant of Emperor Seiwa.

Minamoto no Yoshimitsu, who spent his childhood at Daito Castle in Omni (present-day Yamanashi prefecture) used to be called Saburo Daito and was—along with his two brothers—a seasoned warrior and a passionate researcher into tactics and strategy. He studied Chinese military techniques and was trained in the Mikkio Dojo near the temple of Enjo. He quickly became a scholar trained in the teaching of the classics of Chinese warfare, i.e. the strategists Sun-Tsu, Sun-bin and Wu-Tsu. He was also an early entomologist or student of insects, and it is said that he came to understand the deep meaning of In-no-Yo by observing and discovering how a spider managed to capture a prey larger than itself. In addition, as an expert with the vertical bambou mouth organ, he was an accomplished musician. And finally, along with other martial arts, he was an exceptional wrestler in the art of **tegoi**

inherited from the Genji which, as you may recall—and surely not by chance—gave rise to today's sumo.

Moreover, of the utmost importance as far as the history of our Aiki art is concerned, the three brothers often roamed the fields after battles—even places of execution—with a modern scholar's scientific coldness. Their aim was to understand the human body's intrinsic, natural functioning and especially how to be able to "manipulate" or stimulate bodies, quite probably to learn about joint-locking and point striking.

One can with probable justification imagine the worst and the most hideous, namely that the three Minamoto brothers quickly became de facto accomplished "mechanics of human or animal carcasses". My apologies for the term, but that's precisely what I think it was. Besides, though historic Japanese Aiki was doubtless based on ancient Chinese Chin-Nah techniques blended with tegoi—in my opinion, the original taboo melting pot—its great formational secret was the work these brothers. And this Aiki was then "finalized"—if one can actually go as far as to use the term—into "modern" Aikido as we know it today. Allow me the indulgence of laughing a little here since, considering Aikido's current structural poverty compared with the abundant wealth and incredible relevance of ancient Aiki (Daito-ryu), it's more the word *degeneracy* that comes to mind!*

* *"I watched Aikido techniques at the Nihon Budokan (the big Tokyo sports arena initially dedicated to combat sports), but I found that those who were demonstrating were doing "soft" techniques that don't work in*

real combat situations. Their partners only take falls as a form of service, and it's as if they're practicing falls. In this way, when you throw your opponent, you cannot train properly unless there is a kind of collusion, and he falls to please you. On the other hand, if your partner makes a "beautiful fall", your techniques will always be "good". In our practice (Daito-ryu), our partners do not fall by themselves: we make throws, and they don't need to decide to fall." Interview with Tokimune Takeda, son of Takeda Sokaku (AikiNews # 72).

More prosaically and without any play on words or imagery in bad taste, we could describe this truly "mechanistic science of the human body" as "the animation of the puppeteer". That is to say, specialists in human kinematics or "giving movement" to a "bone framework without upsetting its muscles and strengths. This science—and it really is a science—has no likeness to a muscular "cause and effect" as described in medical anatomy either. In fact, it's curiously closer to the work of a cartoon designer who works on his first draft wire-like sketches. In other words, Aikido is a kind of "pantographic motricity" since it's fundamentally work on the bones. Now, a pantograph is a set of hinged and jointed rods that reproduces the movements of a draughtsman's hands so the "pantograph" notion here is just a useful image since, in the case of Aikido, the reality is human bone (skeleton) and cartilage.

Besides, didn't Morihei Ueshiba repeat, "Aikido is learned with one's bones", thus the secret of this concise definition is at last revealed in all it cold and original splendour. Before this, his students thought that all you had to do to become strong as a tiger, was to work hard like a tiger! Minamoto no Yoshimitsu became, along with his two fellow carcass bio-animators, great mechanists of human "pantography" or what one could also and more simply call specialists in "the mechanics of dead men".* And that's the origin of the Aiki rule that would have us make Aikido movements on or by the bones—and not the muscles.

"You can't do that unless you have studied the construction of the human body as a whole, can you?
Takeda [Tokimune Sensei]: That's right. When the youngest grandson of Emperor Seiwa, Shinra Saburo Yoshimitsu, went to Oshu (the northeastern district of Japan), he studied human anatomy through dissection, and this was the origin of Daito-ryu. He stayed at a place called Daito, and called himself Saburo of Daito. This is where the name Daito comes from. It was passed down through generations of the Takeda family since we are also descendants of the Emperor Seiwa. Our techniques do no allow openings for our enemies." (Stanley A. Pranin, Aiki News #88 – Interview with Tokimune Takeda - 1991)

This allows us to to understand a whole slew of surprising and completely new implications concerning our usual way of thinking. That is to say, rules that tell one not to to concern oneself with the flesh or with techniques that function on the pulley and "hydraulic" principles, the art of power multiplication through pistons or transfers of forces, and so on. Also on lever principles, the principles of Kyusho, the principles of (opponent) imbalances—high, low, lateral, rotating, focused—or the principles of putting under tension and the technical principles of bracing and of serial joint connections. And finally, the principles of stops, extensions, reversals, rotations (use of torque) and extensions and reductions, or of propagation of forces, and so on.

The composite art resulting from this cross-breeding of eclectic but highly specialized knowledge was then compiled under the appelation "**Takeda-no-Heiho**". The name Takeda comes from when Minamoto Yoshikiyo, one of Takeda Yoshimitsu's sons, settled in the Takeda area in Kai province near the Koma mountain, today the Yamanashi administrative district, eastern part of Chubu region. In this regard, it's perhaps significant that the name "Daito-ryu" means "The Great East". The Chubu region lies on the westerly border of the megacity of Tokyo, capital city of Kofu, and this was around **the 1150s** when the current megapolis of Tokyo was still just a mosquito-infested marsh dotted with small villages. From then on, the clan adopted the name of **Kai-Takeda-Genji** or clan "**Kai-Takeda**", later simplified to **Takeda**.

Another source of the In-Yo-Ho art—still sometimes mentioned today—is the "The School of the Great Sabre" (Goto-Daito-ryu), an art founded later by Goto Tamanemon Tadayoshi (1644-1736) and a multidisciplinary martial arts school of the Aizu clan. However, I couldn't find much information about this individal because of the complete destruction of the clan's archives after the wars at the end of the Edo period and beginning of the Meiji restoration. I can only presume that he was probably a famous seventeenth-century fencing master of the clan who further developed the art of Takeda-no-Heiho at the time. This supposition would, of course, in no way undermine the importance of what we have just learned—quite the opposite, in fact.

In any event, as is the way of the world, Takeda-no-Heiho was not destined to continue undivided for ever, and—as we are about to see—its schism was ultimately to lead to Aikido as we know it today.

THE GREAT HISTORICAL DIVIDE
- In the year 1573 on the death of the famous generalissimo **Takeda Shingen***, heir of the Minamoto and thus also a direct descendant of the Emperor Seiwa, the novel and aristocratic art of Takeda-no-Heiho split apart.

> *As a point of information, Takeda Shingen was the cinematic hero in the famous Kurosawa film *Kagemusha*.

This innovative martial art divided into two distinct branches. The first branch was the arts of **Takeda-ryu*** taught to the elite of the **Kuroda** and **Matsudaira** clan in the former province of Echizen (Fukui/Kanazawa), central Japan, on the Sea of Japan side, southwest coast of Honshu. In fact, **Takeda Nobutora**, leader of the Takeda clan who died in the same year as his son Shingen, had entrusted the "family scroll" (a kind of family register) to **Takeda Nobutomo**, his ninth son. The scroll was then entrusted to **Takeda Katsuchiyo** who later went to Echizen province where, according to the Nippon-Budo-Jitsen, he imparted his knowledge to the Kuroda clan.

It should be noted for the record that the Kuroda clan was closely linked to the **Tokugawa** on one hand and, on the other, to the **Toyotomi**. **Kuroda Yoshitaka**, also called Kuroda Kanbei—and later, since he was a christian, "Don Simeon"—

was one of Toyotomi Hideoshi's famous generals at the time. But it's of particular note that a certain **Matsudaira Motoyasu**, born Takechiyo, changed his name with the approval of the Emperor in 1566 to become... the no lesser, **Tokugawa Ieyasu**. And that one of his five girls, O-Roku-no-Kata, was born out of Ieyasu's relationship with lady Nagaharu from the clan... **Kuroda**! Moreover, although it was never proved, to facilitate becoming shogun, the latter declared itself a direct descendant of the illustrious **Minamoto**, and thus an Imperial descendant of the **Genji** princes.

This bending of the truth did not, however, prevent him coming to power in 1603 after the decisive Battle of Sekigahara. And, from there, the establishment of the unrivaled government of the Tokugawa Shoguns in Japan, which lasted for over two hundred and fifty years. In that regard, the **Toyotomi** were finally eliminated during the 1615 fall of the citadel of Osaka, the last bastion of the southern provinces. You can read about it in my (French) saga *L'Épée Reine*, which retraces this exciting historical turning point for Japan as an epic. It is published by Éditions de l'Eveil, but reissued in two volumes under the titles of *L'Épée Reine* (volume I) and *The Dove of Osaka* (Volume II);

---

* Takeda-ryu has Master Nakamura Hisashi as Soke. Today, we also use the term Nakamura-Ha to designate his school, which is grouped under the name of Nihon Sobudo-Kai. Abroad, the school of Master Maroto (Maroto-Ha) tries to perpetuate this tradition as the Kobilza-Ha association...

The second branch of Takeda-no-Heiho was the arts of **Daito-ryu** or Dai-to-ryu (The School of the Great East), but this is the modern name since, between the sixteenth and nineteenth century, it was called the art of **O-Shiki-Uchi** (御式内) according to venerable protocol*. It was also called **O-Tome-Bujutsu** (御留武術) meaning "clan-specific warrior art", **Goten-Jutsu** (御殿術), literally meaning the technique of the honourable palace, and also **Denchu-Saho** (殿中作法), the etiquette inside the palace. (source: Daitokai International (大東流合気武道大東会) and finally, **Daito-ryu Aiki-jujutsu**.

In all these expressions formerly used to designate the arts of Daito-ryu, the word "protocol" or "etiquette"—like the word "palace", for that matter—mean good manners taught for court life in the castles. And that explains the preservation of characteristics of the kneeling work in suwari-waza (shikko) in Aiki techniques.

** The term "protocol" included, of course, the savoir-vivre and the usual customs in private residences or castles (already a "**Do**" in a way), but especially the "know-how of defense" and its associated martiality. Thus one can find the term "Ushiki-Uchi-ryu" (于城内流 (from memory), or "the school of the interior of the palace". It appears that the term "protocol" was in fact a kind of indirect code-name for the secret knowledge of "clan-specific" Aiki-jujutsu. Katsuyuki Kondo talks about it elsewhere: "... at the time of the Meiji Restoration, sword arts were more popular than jujutsu since jujutsu was just beginning to be practiced then. Oshikiuchi, the palace art, was an exception, of course. (Interview with Tokimune Takeda: Aiki News #87). And further on: "These techniques which were so obviously studied for use in the palace are called "oshikiuchi". In the old days when you passed into the Edo castle obanbeya—a large room in a castle in which only distinguised people were allowed to enter—all of your swords were taken away. Everyone,*

except for those nobles with either the title of Suke or Kami (lord) at the end of their names who were allowed to keep their swords and short knives, had to surrender all of their swords. Daito-ryu was the art used during that period. In addition you had to use shikko (knee-walking) in front of the family of the Shogun. This is why in Daito-ryu we practice shikko a great deal. Shikko is particular to Daito-ryu." Interview with Tokimune Takeda (AikiNews #87).

Or according to Kondo Sensei: "About eight hundred years ago, there was a man named Shinra Saburo Yoshimitsu, who resided in a mansion known as "Daito", and he is considered to be the founder of Daito-ryu. His art was then transmitted through the Minamoto family line and then to their descendants, the Takeda family at Kai, present-day Yamanashi Prefecture. After that it was handed down through the Takeda family as a gotenjutsu or martial art for use inside the palace. In addition to this line, during the reign of the fourth Tokugawa Shogun, Ietsuna (1641-1680; shogun 1651-1680), Masayuki Hoshina of the Aizu clan, the fourth son of Hidetada, entered Edo castle as an instructor to the shogunal family and completed development of an art that became known as oshikiuchi." (Stanley A. Pranin interview with Katsuyuki Kondo (<u>AikiNews (1)</u>).

And, again according to Tokimune Takeda:" ...Knee walking (shikko in suwari-waza) is a Daito-ryu expertise. Hanza handachi techniques are also based on knee walking and are used against sudden attacks when seated. Techniques that start in a seated position and end up with the practitioner standing, only exist in Daito-ryu. Other classic martial arts have techniques for controlling the adversary while seated, but it's only in Daito-ryu that you learn how to throw your standing enemy in five direction while in a seating position. We use the term Goho which signifies "the five directions" so the technique is called Gohonage. In combat, you throw your enemy in one of the five directions: to the front, to the rear, right and left, and centrally, the centre being the space you occupy. This kind of technique is unique to Daito-ryu. Equally well, there are five-directional throws associated with Ikkajo, Nikajo, and Sankajo, the series of Daito-ryu in Ikkyo, Nikyo and Sankyo." (Stanley A. Pranin, AikiNews #87 – Interview with Tokimune Takeda - 1991)

Effectively, it is the use of these postures that clearly proves the aristocratic—rather than popular—origins of Aiki. For it was the nobles who needed to be able to neutralize adversaries while in these positions or during the knee walking (shikko*) officially imposed by strict protocol. Certainly not the common people who only needed ground fighting techniques (ne-waza). One also comes across the name "**Go-shikinai**", but I'm afraid I don't have the translation so perhaps it is an appellation coming from the Shinto shrines classified as "Shikinai" or related to court rituals (Engishiki). For the moment, however, I do not have any valid explanations for these different appelations.

* "Anyway, whatever you do, shikko (work on the knees) is important. In the case I mentioned earlier when you were allowed to carry only a short knife, many incidents occurred. The hanza handachi were the techniques which they used to deal with those situations." (Interview with Tokimune Takeda (AikiNews # 87).

This art—or versions of it—were taught to the elite of the Aizu clan. Legend has it that, after the disastrous defeat of the Takeda during the 1573 Battle of Nagashino against Oda Nobunaga and Tokugawa Ieyasu—the famous first battle of swords against the muskets—a surviving member of the Takeda family, Takeda Kunitsugu, fled to the Aizu clan. Faithful to the lineage of the great Takeda Shingen, they offered him a fiefdom, and—in return—he taught the clan the secret art in question. This would explain the transfer of the Takedas' knowledge to the Aizu. However, the Aizu clan was under the authority of Lord Hidetada, also affiliated to Tokugawa and whose mother was born in the Saigo family. The latter, vassals of the Aizu, also benefited from this teaching and even obtained the privilege of having a sort of exclusivity and the duty of transmitting the art to the next generations of Aizu. And that explains why we sometimes come across "Saigo-Ha-Takeda-ryu-Aiki-bujutsu" as a name for this art.

The Tokugawa shoguns eventually ordered the Aizu clan to train their personal guards in this "secret battle art of the Takeda-Saigo castles". And so it was that the school of "the interior of the castle" entered—along with the Shoguns' official sword school "Edo-Yagyu-Shin-Kage ryu"*—into the pantheon of Japanese martial arts through Saigo tutors.

This development took place in correlation with the art of swordmanship, linked to the **Ono-ha Itto-ryu** school from the 1650s. It is important to be quite precise about this since it's very important and one of the sources of Daito-ryu movements, and thus of Aikido itself. For example, the current Kendo teaching patterns—the katas—also come from the **Ono-ha Itto-ryu** school along with those of hokushin itto-ryu, shindo musen-ryu, and jiki shin kage-ryu. In fact, since that time, Takeda-ryu and Ono-ha school were always taught simultaneously, and Takeda Sokaku, an excellent fencer whom we will talk about later, ended up including the still secret practice of this sword school while spreading Daito-ryu during the twentieth century. And this, despite the recommendations of his master Tanomo who wanted to dissuade him.

*"Edo-Yagyu-Shin-Kage ryu", so named for the simple reason the Shogun lived in Edo and this swordsmanship art was founded by Yagyu Munenori (1571-1646), the great fencer and great contemporary rival of Miyamoto Musashi.

These two great technical ancestors of Aikido—**Daito-ryu** and **Ono-ha Itto-ryu**—simplifying here since, as you're beginning to understand, it's not actually as straightforward as that—were basically codified as being "**The Yin-Yang Technique of Unification**". Or, to better clarify things for our Western minds—little able to grasp the meaning of such a codification—I would define it as "The Yin-Yang Technique of Zero Unification" where "zero" is the goal to reach.

In Japanese, this was called "Aiki-no-jutsu". And this, despite the fact the word "**Aiki**"—"energy, will or means of unification" replacing the term "Use of Yin and Yang Complements"—only appeared as such quite late in Japanese historical literature. In fact, it was almost certainly introduced by **Takeda Takumi-no-Kami**—also known as **Takeda Soemon** (1758-1853)—Takeda Sokaku's own grandfather.

So, as we have seen earlier, these techniques were taught—in series and very discreetly—from the same original source, that of the famous **Shinra Saburo Minamoto no Yoshimitsu**—to the respective social elites of the clan heirs, underlings, or Minamoto allies. Then later to shogunate court authorties.

For the record here, listed below is the transmission time line of the Takedas' knowledge right up to today's Daito-ryu.

Shinra Saburo Minamoto Yoshimitsu
Takeda Yoshikiyo
Takeda Kiyomitsu
Takeda Nobuyoshi
Takeda Nobumitsu
Takeda Nobumasa
Takeda Nobutoki

Takeda Tokitsuna
Takeda Nobumune
Takeda Nobutake
Takeda Nobunari
Takeda Nobuhara
Takeda Nobumitsu
Takeda Nobushige
Takeda Nobumori
Takeda Nobumasa
Takeda Nobunawa
Takeda Nobutora
Takeda Kunitsugu
Takeda Chikara
Takeda Nobutsugu
Takeda G.
Takeda Y.
Takeda S.
Takeda Y.
Takeda Sôemon
Takeda Sokichi
TAKEDA SOKAKU
TAKEDA TOKIMUNE
Takeda Munekiyo (Aizu)
Takeda Muneyasu
Takeda Munemitsu
Takeda Hitoshi (Rubeshibe)

Using the same source—namely the Takumakai, one of the major Daito-ryu Aiki-jujutsu organizations—and equally accurately, it is possible to retrace contemporary history through the acknowledged successors of Takeda Sokaku's art. They are listed below with the start date of their apprenticeship.

1905 - Shimoe Hidetaro from Hokushin Itto-Ryu Genbukan
1905 - Harada Shinzo
1908 - Oi Takijiro from Shinkage-ryu
1909 - Mikami Tomikji of Kito-ryu and Tenjin Shinryo-ryu
1911 - Kodama Takayoshi from Shindo Munen-ryu
1913 - Horikawa Yasumune
1914 - Horikawa Kodo from Kodokai => Inoue Yusuke & Okamoto Seigo
1914 - Sagawa Yukitoshi
1915 - Yoshida Kotaro => Yoshida Kenji from Yanagi-ryu
1915 - Ueshiba Morihei => Aikido
1928 - Matsuda Toshimi => Okuyama Toshiharu (Hakko-Ryu)
1929 - Mae Kitutaro
1936 - Tonedate Masao (menkyo-kaiden)
1936 - Hisa Takuma (menkyo-kaiden) => Takumakai
1936 - Yoshimura Yoshiteru
1936 - Nakatsu Heisaburo => then Chiba Tsugutak & Makita Kanichi ... (Shikoku branch)
1936 - Yamamoto Kakugi (Mugen Shinto-ryu)

In addition, one can cite the following:

19-- Suzuki Shinpachi (Kyoju Dairi)
1957 - Kondo Katsuyuki (menkyo-kaiden)
1962 - Mori Hakaru (Kyoju Dairi), Kobayashi Kiyohiro, Kawabe Takeshi, Utsunomiya Mamoru, Araki Masunori, Sato Hideyuki, Kobayashi Takashi ... (listed heads of the Takumakai organization or

affiliates. Since the list is long and laborious, we offer our apologies to those not mentioned.
1970 - Kato Shigemitsu
1972 - Nakamura Naoshita

TOWARDS AIKI-JUJUTSU

- It is of critical importance to recognize today's Aikido stems directly from Daito-ryu Aiki-jujutsu, the final name and ultimate form of the second and—socially speaking—very elitist branch of the original Takeda-no-Heiho. This is the Minamoto-Takeda-Aizu-Saigo branch ("Aiki-no-jutsu") or what was, for a while, known as **Oshiki-Uchi** (after the 1651 reform by Hoshina Masayuki, a grandson of no less than Ieyasu Tokugawa) and, as such, intrinsically linked to Japanese power of the Edo period.

So much for the birth of the art, and now, on to Aiki-jujutsu. This very particular teaching of "The Art of Defense of the Court" would be continued until the dissolution of the Aizu clan in 1868. In fact, the Aizu clan—allied with the shogun Tokugawa—would perish on that date at the decisive battle of Shirakawaguchi in the war between the shogunate forces and those of the Emperor Meiji. Unfortunately for the clan and Aiki-jujutsu, they were decimated, dissolved and annihilated, and their possessions and property—including, sad to say, their archives—were tragically bombarded, burned and destroyed. In short, a clean slate! Or almost...

After these events, the art was renamed "Daito-ryu" because Takeda Kunitsugu, an ancient descendant

(Takeda) of Minamoto no Yoshimitsu ("Oshiki-Uchi" branch), had been obliged to change **his** name following the fall of his domain in 1582—again after a memorable battle. He then, according to usual procedure in old Japan, called himself Hisanosuke Daito from the name of the place where he had taken refuge. And it is the name "Daito" which was—once again—taken up by the famous Sokaku **Takeda** to name the Aiki-jujutsu art at the end of the nineteenth century. He had intially called it the "**Yamamoto** School" since that appelation's calligraphic characters read the same way as "**Daito**". However, as Kisshomaru Ueshiba said one day in an interview with Aiki News*, "that never had anything to do with the reactionary political concept of "Dai-toa kyoeiken no chiseigakuteki kosatsu" (大東亜共栄圏地政学的考察) or "Geopolitical Consideration of the Co-Prosperity Sphere of Greater East Asia", which the Japanese colonial military wanted to put in place in the 1930-1940s*.

* *Aiki News No.79 of January 1989 for those of you who are fond of history. Kisshomaru Ueshiba speaks of the "Greater East Asia Co-Prosperity Sphere", which at about the same time, was a Meiji era idea initiated with great brutality during the Showa era (1926- 1945) to create an autonomous bloc of the "East Asian continent". Also called Pan-Asia, it was directed and exploited by an all-powerful militiarized Japan which denounced with the height of cynicism, the Western countries' continued colonial policy. However, the actual result of this political entity was the systematic plunder of the countries then occupied by Japan (1940: Operation "Golden Lily") led by the imperial princes Yasuhito Chichibu and... Tsuneyoshi Takeda (1909-1992), cousin of Emperor Hiro Hito. Tsuneyoshi Takeda was exonerated from criminal prosecution after the war by the Americans because of his Imperial affiliation, and ... named future chairman of the organizing committee of the 1964 Summer Olympics in Tokyo and the 1972 Winter Olympics in Sapporo (Rather woolly, to say the least ?).*

So there you have it: the historical muddle of clans and subclans and the transmissions from master to master during the "Middle Ages" of Japan. What emerges from this brief presentation is that, in general, the history of this martial arts branch—under the name Aiki-jujutsu for hundreds of years—allowed a slow evolution and maturing of this specific form of one-to-one combat's strategic art, much later to be baptized "Aiki". So it was thanks to the composition of the genius Morihei Ueshiba, that this maturing process finally led to Aikido as we know it today. And "it is recognized" that Aikido did emerge from ancestral Aiki techniques, at least to the extent that most practitioners believe they know them.

But now let's turn our attention back to the pre-contemporary era of Sokaku Takeda, an era which is itself not necessarily much clearer anyway.

BUT WHO WAS SOKAKU TAKEDA? - **Sokaku Takeda** was born on October 10th 1859 in the Takeda Aizu mansion in Oike in the present-day Fukushima region on the Pacific coast, some 150 km north-east of Tokyo as the crow flies. He was the second son of samurai Sokichi Takeda, a famous Aizu clan sumo wrestler who rose to the rank of Oseki, the highest sumo rank before the ultimate rank of "Yokozuna". He was also a renowned warrior with prodigious strength, having distinguished himself highly in the last battles involving the pro-shogunal Aizu clan at the time of the Meiji Restoration. Sokichi Takeda's father was Soemon Takeda, who was

a master of Daito-ryu and an expert in the Shinto religion among the Saigo, and a very distant descendant of the original Takeda.

Takeda Sokaku, the grandson of Soemon, was a child of war with a curious character—adventurous, untimely, exuberant, playful and reckless—and a diminutive but agile, acrobatic and fast body. In fact, he was said to "be able to jump eleven feet in a single breath ", that is to say, for a little man one metre fifty tall and weighing fifty-two kilo, to jump almost three metre sixty in a moment and in any direction! On top of that, he was left-handed with an ambidextrous tendency—hence his ease for fencing with both hands. He was also a little braggart of a man in his youthful glory, had a clear aversion to injustice and, despite certain talents for verbal sophistication and the theatre of life, had an equal repugnance for literature, and therefore for writing.

In his early youth, he was called "the ugly little monkey" by the villagers and, despite his many qualities, remained quite illiterate all his life. After the death of his brother—a Shinto priest himself—his father, tried to get him into the Shinto priesthood in his youth. However, the child did not succeed because of his weakness in literature and calligraphy which he hated, and this apparently discouraged him.

On the other hand, brought up with his father's good name, he was soon a gifted sumo wrestler. In fact, as a teenager but without his father's permission, he won great prizes against famous, even professional wrestlers in the various seasonal or one-off festivals in Aizu territory. Besides, the clan was also renowned throughout Japan for its sumo as well as for the art of the spear and the javelin. In fact, the turbulent Sokaku, who too often ridiculed the best wrestlers, was over-gifted in sumo to the point of being finally banned from the championship by his own father. In his exasperation and tired of being unable to calm his son down, he eventually steered him towards the art of stick fighting and fencing. He authorized him to go and study Jikishin Kage-ryu with the famous master Sakakibara Kenkichi in Tokyo*, whose main technique lay in the mastery of jodan, high guard fencing little used at the time. Sokaku then applied himself so diligently that he later received the menkyo-kaiden, the school's highest possible diploma.

But let's go back: we were still in 1873, and Sokaku was only thirteen!

* *The phrase* **"Dojo of Hell"** *actually dates from this time and was used to decribe* **Sakakibara Kenkichi's** *uncompromising fencing dojo. It was later revived—the Japanese love copied/pasted in their own way, genre "It's me who invented"—to designate Morihei Ueshiba's (first) Tokyo Kobukan Dojo. And that's something that few aikidoka know about today.*

He was also a student of Toma Shibuya, a prestigious master of the traditional Aizu "Ono-ha Itto-ryu" swordsmanship school as well as being a student and protégé of the equally-famous master Shunzo Masano Monoi of the Kyoshin Meichi ryu school in Sakai City, Osaka.

Thanks to his passion, training and talent, Sokaku Takeda quickly developed into an outstanding swordsman and, at the outset, devoted himself to the teaching of fencing. However, because of the social revolution taking place in Meiji-era Japan (from 1868), that kind of teaching had become somewhat out-of-date. The Meiji era was in full swing with the authoritarian suppression of the social and economic standing of the warrior class, and even the abolition of the former feudal society's four "classes". For several centuries, these four social groups—samurai, artisans, peasants and merchants—had not only been the backbone of a system that ensured state stability in Tokugawa Japan, but also the sustainable and autonomous basis of its martial law for centuries.

So it was that, at the beginning of the twentieth century, Takeda Sokaku—nicknamed Aizu-no-Kotengu or "the little demon of Aizu"—after becoming a formidable swordsman in several fencing styles, and later custodian of the ancient secrets of the Minamoto (Genji-Minamoto-Kai-Takeda-Aizu-Saigo), began to travel through Japan on a "martial arts pilgrimage".

He criss-crossed the regions from famous dojo to famous dojo, proposing a fight with the local master or challenging a particular school. In fact, so serious was he in his research that he even went to Okinawa Island to gauge the capabilities of the famous "Chinese hand" fighters. These were practitioners of "kara-te", later referred to as "the art of the empty hand", and arts he deemed inferior to those of sword and spear.

In general, he had to fight the best students of a particular master before he could hope to actually face off against the master himself and, even then, the outcome was not always certain. But when he had proved himself in a dojo he visited, he was generally allowed to impart his knowledge for some time while receiving food and shelter. Sometimes, on his departure, the master would offer him a small gratuity to help him continue his research. And, at best, the master's letter of introduction to the master of another dojo he knew in another locality, sometimes at the other end of Japan.

Many of this kind of "pilgrim" had an abrupt end to their life after entering a dojo, without anyone ever hearing anything more about them. In effect, these truth-seekers were homeless, often anonymous, completely unregistered and, in any case, no one really knew what was going on in the dojos of that time, much less behind the scenes.

But Sokaku Takeda survived, won practically all his challenges, traveled virtually the length and breadth of Japan and, according to reports, even indulged in several exploits against armed gangs or groups of bandits. Sometimes he escaped death by a hair's breadth with a stroke of genius or just by chance, proof that no one is invulnerable. One such example was the incident at Inawashiro, the town of his maternal Kurokoshi family, in Fukushima Prefecture. On this occasion, he killed several armed men in an ambush on a bridge in the middle of the night. Mistaking him for someone else, they had attacked him by surprise, but he ducked and dived in the dark, fought and "cut some legs" before finally jumping into the river to escape.

Then there was the Aizubange-Yanaizu pass incident when he rid the steep mountain road of the presence of three bandits who took hostages for ransom. He was travelling alone on the mountain road when he met the three men who had set a trap for him, but they were defeated by his close-combat techniques and use of a wide range of iron weapons, doubtless formidable in his expert hands. He left them for dead, pushing their dying bodies into the valley, but the villagers found them in a pitiful state at the bottomof a ravine two days later, two still alive, and one dead. The villagers—now rid of the bandits—were jubilant, cooked smoked rice and red beans, and had a celebration party.

Then there was the famous episode of the road under construction between Tokyo and Sendai, three hundred kilometres north of the capital, when Sokaku Takeda found himself up against fifty road workers who also practiced organized banditry in their spare time. They were armed with swords and spears, but he defeated his many opponents, killed ten of them in the fight, and was himself wounded more than thirty times. He was rescued at the last minute by the police, indicted since he was carrying an illegal sword-cane, but cleared after a month of investigation and, if truth be told, detention. This event firmly established his notoriety as a fighter and would, once he was cleared, allow him to teach a range of civil servants, such as police, judges, public prosecutors and even officials of the time, thus greatly enhancing his address book.

There were also incidents in Fukushima, where the authorities found the bodies of several outlaws and bandits in the vicinity of Sokaku's area of activity. It was thought it could only be his doing—doubtless stress-testing his art—but without ever knowing for sure what it was really all about, and without being able to build a case against him.

Finally, there was the Hakodate incident in Hokkaido. This northernmost part of Japan was very wild at the time since it was a region of "pioneers" who were progressively colonizing it with all the anarchy one can imagine. And it was here, in this atmosphere of the true "Japanese Wild West", that Sokaku was officially appointed the Hakodate court bodyguard, and more specifically of the public prosecutor, Shigemori Fujita, who had summoned him for this position.

Sokaku then had some disagreements with "Mo's group"—a gang named after their leader, Tsunekichi Morita—which was directly attacking the legal activities of this court. Attacked by five or six bandits from Mo's band as he was leaving the public baths, he seriously wounded them or sent them packing thanks to his wet towel that he used as a whip. Later, when Mo's group rounded up more than two hundred minions to get rid of Sokaku without more ado, he defied advisors who had suggested he flee the region. His response to their worries was to say, "... Know it that in the evening, I will go down to their den and I will scatter the ground with their bodies". No sooner said than done, he openly went to Morita's house at night, armed only with his sword, but was recognized at the entrance by one of the thug's bodyguards who challenged him. The bodyguard, a former police sergeant turned security agent for Mo, then introduced him directly to the gang leader. The dispute was clearly spelled out in front of the boss, and he acknowledged the "error" of Sokaku's five attackers at the exit of the bathing establishment. Sokaku then left calmly, but the trouble they'd had and the thirst for revenge against the court's bodyguard lingered on in Morita's men.

It was finally the intervention and the negotiation of Hakodate's police department director with Morita which put a stop to the illegal activities of the Mo group against the court and its employees. But only on one condition, namely that the dreadful Sokaku Takeda definitively leave Hokkaido. The reason given for his departure from the region was that it was 1904 {well into the Meiji era} and his "mission" of restoring order had been accomplished.

So it was that Sokaku Takeda—after all his epic adventures—began to teach and finally passed on his secrets to numerous students including... none other than Morihei Ueshiba.

It's important to note here that Takeda Sokaku had been entrusted by **Saigo Chikasama Tanamo,*** his master of Daito-ryu (Oshiki-uchi had become Aiki-jujutsu) to reveal his art to the outside world, thus outside a very closed circle of select members of the Saigo-Aizu clan. In order to show that the time to teach sword fighting, to fight against all odds, and to return to the bushi (warrior) or samurai era was truly over, his

Master conveyed his hope using the following poetic lines:

"Beat the flowing water

leave no trace on the water"

* Saigo Chikasama Tanamo (1829-1905) was one of the ministers of the Aizu clan during its zenith at Aizu Castle in Shirakawa. One of the few survivors of the annihilation of the Aizu clan with Soemon, grandfather of Sokaku, he became a prominent Shinto priest—the only respectable way of salvation for opponents of the defeated Emperor, except, of course, that of ritual suicide . He is also known by his name of Shinto superior at the Tsutsukowake (Fukushima) temple: **Hoshino Chikanori**.

THE MEIJI ERA

- So Sokaku did not try to fight the wind or "beat the water" of his time, but busied himself by allowing the modernizing events of the Meiji era to carry him along. So it was that he began to teach what previously was not taught—the Aiki Jujutsu of the Saigos—and he did it with zeal and perseverance.

However, Sokaku never taught in a dojo of his own but, as before, continued to travel across Japan teaching Daito-ryu. Thanks to the list of his students in his personal account-books (twenty volumes of his "Eimei-Ryoku" which he meticulously kept like a notary), we can see he had considerable authority right up to very influential circles in early twentieth-century Japan. We also know from these records exactly what he taught and to whom, for how long, for what sums of money, and up to what level since he noted it all down scrupulously.

Sokaku didn't teach everything he knew to everyone, but rather, bearing in mind the extent of the student's learning, various abilities, morphology, social standing or even the state of his wallet, he only taught what he considered suitable. It appears in his documents that, contrary to what one might think, Sokaku Takeda was neither greedy nor rolling in money, and did not overcharge for his prodigious knowledge. On the other hand, he was extremely demanding when it came to the choice of who could have even the slightest idea of the knowledge he held, eliminating all those who were—in his opinion—morally or for other reasons, not worthy of it.

We discover that Morihei Ueshiba, although he was then painstaking and deeply spiritually invested with Master Sokaku Takeda, did not study with him for unbroken or, above all, for long periods at any one time. Almost certainly, this was difficult at the time, but the records of 1915-1916, 1922 and 1931 often show ten days of intensive training in a row. According to witnesses, however, he did nonetheless build a dojo and a makeshift residence for Sokaku in Hokkaido and, in 1916, offered to let him stay in his house while he was away. And, according to accounting records, he spent a considerable amount of money to follow his teaching in his youth, especially between their milestone meeting in 1915 and 1919, and then later until 1937.

But it's all relative since, on the other hand, we also know Ueshiba intensely followed his Master in the

Hokkaido region and then, as an assistant, during his wanderings. And that means a lot.

We also know that Sokaku mainly taught Morihei only certain types of Daito-ryu techniques, apparently because of Ueshiba's physical build since he was a small man and, at that time, not very powerful.

All the same, Takeda Sokaku had a profound esteem for Morihei Ueshiba Morihei, and thought he had a very promising future in this discipline. Unfortunately the relationship subsequently clouded over, and this was probably for political reasons (licence or teaching direction) or over money problems related to royalties due to Takeda. Or even quarrels involving the fair sex : "Ah, Xanthippe! As Socrates had exclaimed to his wife long ago." But, of course, all that is just the stuff of rumors almost unverifiable today because taboos, once again, are legion. So, perhaps the reader can go and find out exactly what hapened. But, of course, without mentioning my name.

Anyhow, according to the few Daito-Ryu experts who were close to or studied with Morihei Ueshiba, and that I was able to meet, Ueshiba Morihei excelled in the art of Daito-Ryu in an absolutely prodigious way. And this, of course, begs the question of what he went on to do with this extraordinary talent.

WHAT EXACTLY DID MORIHEI DO?

- n fact, Morihei Ueshiba began by actually teaching "Daito-ryu Aiki-jujutsu"—and under that name—until Takeda Sokaku forbade it because he had not given him the proper licence, the menkyo-kaiden or "full transmission certificate". It was 1922 and Sokaku had only awarded him a kyoju-dairi diploma, that is to say, literally, "professor by proxy". Yet old pre-war photos of Morihei Ueshiba in action leave absolutely no doubt as to the Daito-ryu root of the techniques, still intact and clearly shown on these documents. This is the case except for the arts of sabre and stick fighting where the origins are, apart from various influences of ryu (schools) we can sometimes only guess at, often very personal to the founder. And this is something I'll talk about later.

In fact, without any authorization whatsoever, Morihei Ueshiba even awarded Daito-ryu-Jujutsu diplomas to at least four of his students: Kenji Tomiki, Minoru Mochizuki, Rinjiro Shirata, and Gozo Shioda.

However, faced with the embarrassment of not being able to officially use the name of Daito-ryu, he gave the art he taught various other names over the years, such as "Ueshiba-juku", then "Ueshiba-ryu-jujutsu" until 1924, "Ueshiba-ryu" from 1925-1926, "Aiki-budo" after 1926. He also used the appelations "Asahi-ryu* jujutsu", "Kobu-budo", and "Aiki-no-michi" with "michi" or the way having the same character and the same meaning as "Do", and with "no" being the Japanese genitive (possesive) grammatical particle.

Asahi-ryu in Osaka: Ueshiba Morihei—until the manu-militaristic arrival of his master Takeda Sokaku who replaced him on the spot—taught the team of counter-terrorism experts at the Asahi newspaper in Osaka. It was a group of various martial arts champions (judo, sumo, and so on) who were in charge of protecting the newspaper, its premises, and its leaders or employees. We must not underestimate this episode of Aikido since, for many reasons, it is of extreme importance. It shows, for example, that even before war, the techniques of Aiki-jujutsu (Daito-ryu) were considered much more efficient than others when it came to civil protection, personal protection, or security protection. This sort of martial arts hierarchy in favour of the art of Aiki had been reversed in the aftermath of the war, a situation that has continue up until today. And if we were to ask ourselves, "why?". Well, that is exactly what we're going to see further on...

Just the same, Aikido—Ueshiba's modern evolution of Takeda Sokaku's art—was not the only offshoot from Daito-ryu, and some of the others are listed below.

1) **Nihon Daito-ryu Aikibudo Daito Kai** which is represented by former direct pupils of Takeda Tokimune (1915-1992), the late Takeda Sokaku's second son. And it is to him that we owe a very large part of the chronicles of his father's life;

2) **Takuma-Kai**, a cultural association, formed by the students of Takuma Hisa (1896-1980). He was a former sumo wrestler and the only disciple that Takeda Sokaku fully recognized by the attribution of a menkyo-kaiden certificate in 1939. As we have seen previously, this is the highest distinction in the old system of Japanese martial arts, certifying a full transmission of the art and therefore the master's acceptance of the pupil's freedom. It was also Takuma Hisa who had the presence of mind and the opportunity to establish a real photographic library of Sokaku techniques. A reference

collection for this organization, it is scrupulously maintained as techniques of "Soden"* in eleven absolutely astonishing books of photographs;

*The **Soden**, created by Takuma Hisa of Takuma-Kai, contains a collection of photographs of Takeda Sokaku's techniques which he managed to take during the time Sokaku was teaching at Osaka's Asahi newspaper (between 1933 and 1939). The story goes that Takuma invited Sokaku take a hot bath after class, and while the teacher's back was being rubbed on the mat and in the dojo, using newspaper materials, the students quickly took pictures of the techniques that had just been demonstrated. It is thanks to their outstanding feat that eleven volumes of photography (exceptional for the time) were compiled of Daito-ryu Aiki-jujutsu techniques. A number of these treasured volumes were also published in Japan: books ten and eleven appeared in a pre-war budo magazine called "Shin Budo" (The New Budo), currently unavailable, of course. In addition, I believe some of the photos were also published in part by Aiki News in 1990. The originals are kept at the headquarters of Takuma-Kai, and the eleven illustrated textbooks were named the "**Soden Waza**". The first six volumes contain techniques learned from Morihei Ueshiba's teaching, and seven to nine contain techniques learned from Takeda Sokaku at the Asahi newspaper dojo (set as he soaked in his steam baths). Book ten is made up of secret arrest techniques of the police, and book eleven is a collection of female self-defense techniques. The **Soden** contains a total of 547 techniques, but according to Hakaru Mori, Takuma-Kai's chairman, there are several hundred other existing techniques that are not accounted for in these books and that are part of Soden. And that's not all because Takuma Hisa has published other books: "Kannagara no Budo" (The Martial Art of Deities), "Joshi Goshinjutsu" (Self defense for Women), not to mention "Ogi Hiden" (The Secrets of Hand-to-Hand Techniques). He himself also made a film about Morihei Ueshiba, and the title was "Ueshiba no Shidofukei" or "Ueshiba's Instructional Techniques".*

*Turning back to **the Asahi newspaper episode**, "In June 1936, an unusual event occured which was to completely reorient the direction of the training at the Asahi dojo where Morihei was teaching". In Hisa's own words, this is what happened. "Sokaku Dai Sensei—the Grand Master Sakaku (Takeda)—suddenly appeared out of nowhere, without any notice or previous invitation. He was diminutive but had brilliant, piercing eyes, and he had a dagger in his belt. Also, he walked while holding a heavy iron rod in his right hand—the kind that only a mountain ascetic can carry. He shouted out, "Greetings to all! Bring me the general manager. I am the professor of Morihei Ueshiba's Aiki-jujutsu, and I am* *called Sokaku Takeda. I have learned that, despite his scant experience, Morihei Ueshiba teaches Aiki-jujutsu here. On the other hand, for the honour of Daito-ryu Aiki-jujutsu, I consider it to be of paramount importance that only good techniques be taught at the Asahi News in front of the eyes of the whole world. So I came down from Hokkaido as soon as possible". And holding his iron pike above his head, he rather pompously said, "And we start the next lesson now".". (Aiki News, Remembering Takuma Hisa by Stanley Pranin – "Sokaku Takeda Arrives in Osaka").*

3) **Kodokai**. This was the branch of Kodo Horikawa (1894-1980). His students themselves formed the organization which later split into two streams: **Daito-ryu Aiki Jujutsu Roppokai** (by Seigo Okamoto (1925-); and **Bukuyokan** (by Katsumi Yonezawa (1937-1999));

4) The branch of **Yukiyosha Sagawa** (1902-1998) who taught in his personal dojo in Kodaira City near Tokyo. He was an amazing character who started Daito-ryu with Sokaku when he was a child, and was destined in mid-century to become Sokaku Takeda's successor in the event his son Tokimune had died in the Pacific War;

5) Korean **Hapkido** of Yon-Sool-Choi;

6) **Hakko-ryu** by Yoshiji Okuyama, a direct student of Matsuda Hosaku, himself a disciple of Sokaku Takeda and a calligraphy expert in charge of writing his Daito ryu mokuroku (certificates and diplomas) and his personal secretary;

7) **Shorinji-Kempo** by Nakano Michiomi, also called in Chinese "So Doshin". Nakano Michiomi was a Daito-ryu pupil of the previous Okuyama master of

Hakko-ryu, and—surprise, surprise—of the Shaolin Temple Kempo masters in China. You must admit this truly amazing turn of history proves that, while history does not repeat itself, it certainly rhymes.

So, on that rather harmonic note, we will now get back to Aikido itself.

THE BIRTH OF AIKIDO

We know that Morihei Ueshiba, after absorbing Daito-ryu knowledge at the side of his master Takeda Sokaku, then used syncretism—a kind of amalgamation—to evolve "Ki no awasekata". As we have seen, this Japanese term expresses the way of **wanting** to synergistically link the different forms of "Ki" together. That is to say, the binding together of an **array of forces**, energy in apparently conflicting directions, into an unambiguous result. A result internal to the body or dynamic and external to it, and one greater than the sum of its original constituents, that can then be more easily used for this or that purpose.

This amalgamation process was continued and accentuated by Morihei Ueshiba's successors who strove to make the practice of Daito-ryu more understandable and revealing. Nonetheless, the practice was still opaque, difficult, and fundamentally extremely dangerous*, and its disclosure, not only rather elitist, but also very technical and destructive into the bargain.

* *"Every Daio-ryu technique is deadly. None of the techniques offers openings to the opponent. Interview with Tokimune Takeda (AikiNews #88)*

However the historical details of Daito-ryu are not easy to unearth, and it must be said that the origins or proofs pertaining to these ancient times were confused, lost, and often destroyed during the conflicts. In addition, the only historical sources which remain were long ago entrusted to the Grand Ise Temple where access is forbidden, except to Shinto priests! I think we can also say today that many of the proofs or details were unwittingly, out of ignorance or stupidity, or—for unknown reasons—deliberately eliminated or "omitted" by many of the instructors who next took up this chain of knowledge.

It must be said here that even the succession of teachers has often functioned rather like the game of Chinese Whispers or Telephone. In this way, the original message—the original technique—was completely distorted and, at the end of the line, even reversed compared to what it was originally. Many revisionisms come from just that: the total or relative misunderstanding of students who believe they have understood and, in turn, pass on notions which are completely false. In general, they say, "Oh yes, but it works!" The problem is that they never ask themselves the question about the conditions or parameters under which their pseudo knowledge works—or doesn't—on others. For example, a Sensei is absolutely never contested by his students in the middle of the mat, quite the opposite, in fact. How then can he vindicate the correctness of his teaching? Another example is that Aikido practitioners work and train as if their movement was perfect and they themselves were invincible. But the reality is that things never happen like that: perfection in the act of combat is absolutely rare—reciprocity demands that—and invincibility almost minimal. In fact, the ten-percent rule states that, in general, one out of ten prey attacked by a super-predator is actually captured.

Well, yes, I admit I'm exaggerating a bit here, but why is failure not an integral part of the emotion in Aikido training? The relative or absolute miscomprehension of students who believe they have understood—and, in turn, pass on completely false notions—is one of the major current problems in Aikido.

In their defense, it must be repeated that founder Ueshiba Morihei's teaching was quite special—almost transcendental—and not really adapted to his young students so their difficulties with it are understandable. A post-war student of the founder and a prestigious developer of Aikido in France, Tamura Sensei, who passed away very recently, spoke earlier of the problem of the early Aikido teaching, and said, "We had extraordinary teaching, but we were blind. And we made our students bear the weight of our ignorance!" (Interview with Tamura Nobuyoshi, the Eagle of Aikido, Tsubaki-Journal, Thursday, September 27, 2007). An official mea culpa and, above all, a very courageous one—so hats off to Tamura Sensei—but a mea culpa that couldn't properly solve the problem of the diminution of the art or bring about its return. So we have to look elsewhere for corroberation, complements, and pieces of the Aiki puzzle... And what a puzzle it is, almost a needle in a haystack!

In his youth, the founder was not only influenced by different apprenticeships, but also he was exposed to them in the most intimate and varied of ways, as he expressed below.

A: "When did you begin the study of martial arts?"
O-Sensei: "At about the age of fourten or fifteen, I first learned Tenshinyo-ryu Jiujitsu from Tokusaburo Tozawa Sensei. Then Kito-ryu, Yagyu-ryu, Aioi-ryu, Shinkage-ryu—all of them forms of jujutsu. However, I thought perhaps there might be a true form of Budo elsewhere. I tried Hozoin-ryu sojitsu and kendo." ("Aikido" by Kisshomaru Ueshiba, Tokyo, Kowado, 1957- Interview with Morihei Ueshiba and Kisshomaru Ueshiba)

But, as I have already mentioned, there were also his "intellectual" relations with the world and history of his time. For example and not without consequence, with the polymath Kumagusu Minataka (1867-1941), who is today considered to be the father of the Japanese environmental movement. Not to mention his relations with the uppermost circles of Japanese power at the time.

There was also—and above all—the profound and intimate relationship he maintained with a new Japanese Shinto religious group with ultra-nationalist and paradoxically pacifist tendencies. This was the Omoto sect, a branch of Shinto called "the teaching of the great origin" and directed by Onisaburo Deguchi—formerly Ueda Kisaburo—and his illiterate mother-in-law, Nao Deguchi. The teachings of this sect and its leaders' personalities marked him very deeply** (*See the note below on the biography of Ueshiba Morihei*). In fact, the founder had the opportunity to participate in a strange expedition with Onisaburo Deguchi to Manchuria in the middle of the Sino-Japanese war. They were looking for—or looking to create—the ancient kingdom of "Shangri-la", one of the historical and mythical ideal worlds of universal peace.

For this adventure on Chinese territory, Morihei Ueshiba (born Moritake) would even adopt a Chinese name, **Wang Shou Kao**. And it is believed that, on this auspicious occasion, he could have found time or the opportunity to make contact with several great masters of Chinese martial arts*, including Pa-koua Chang or "Baguazhang".

**In this regard, Chinese sources (Hong Kong Chinese Martial Arts Association or HKCMAAL) name masters Yen Dehua and Gao Yisheng. Ueshiba Morihei later became the martial arts advisor of the Mongolia-based Japanese organization Shimbuden (Dojo) and Kenkyoku University. The Chinese archives, or perhaps the Chinese masters, no doubt would have much to teach us in the matter of the contribution of their arts to Ueshiba Morihei during this long period when he was so close to them in Manchuria (He also made brief stays—often secret—mandated by the (Japanese) power in place).*

Pa-Koua which dates back to the eighteenth century, has the distinction of being a very complete Chinese martial art. It has a naturalist philosophy based on personal refocusing, and includes fighting techniques, meditation techniques and shamanism—all very close to the Aikido founder's poles of interest. Pa-koua movements are often based on rotating or spiral principles and, although we'll probably never know for sure, it's therefore reasonable to assume the founder's techniques underwent a technical crossover—practical, reflexive, and theoretical. This is just another case of where the true history of Aikido's development—correctly as it turns out—finds its way back to China. Further credence for this supposition is provided by those who knew him at the time. They recalled that, after his journey in Mongolia—in addition to and in support of Daito-ryu techniques—his forms of work had an astonishing resemblance to the Baguazhang ways of displacements or control.

And that is the story of what happened "before 1942". However, the reader must bear in mind that I have only traced a few broad historical lines, and even they are in summary form and thus obviously barely sketched out. In any event, this brings us to the question of just where this martial art of Morihei Ueshiba was headed for.

**For the official biography of Morihei Ueshiba, there are a multitude of sources—curiously always more or less similar and stereotyped—so, if you want to look no further, we refer you to them. But if you're looking for something better, I can best quote Peter Goldsbury here for his foresight in this matter, when he writes, " Biographies of Morihei Ueshiba tend to be episodic, rather like the scenes in a Kabuki play. The drama starts in Tanabe with his education in a Shingon Buddhist terakoya—affiliated elementary school—and a rootless life after his military service. It then suddenly shifts to Hokkaido where, in a desolate environment, he is almost single-handedly forming a rugged farming community. The discovery of Sokaku Takeda follows—along with lengthy training sessions—and then he is off again, back to Tanabe to look after his sick father's wellbeing. The plot veers off yet again here, and Ueshiba goes miles out of his way to Ayabe to meet a certain Onisaburo Deguchi who, it is supposed, will be able to do something about his father. In a *sense, the visit is fruitless since his father is already dead before Ueshiba finally arrives back in Tanabe. But then the scene dramatically changes once more, and off he goes again—this time with his family—to Ayabe where he will be Reverand Deguchi's bodyguard. And the rest is, as they say, history. Except for one thing: it's not history. Because what we really have here is a biography-hagiography hybrid organized to reveal a certain truth about Morihei Ueshiba. Sunadomari's biography tails off after he's made his main point, namely that the most central fact about Aikido was Ueshiba's meeting and training with Onisaburo Deguchi. On the other hand, while Kisshomaru Ueshiba's biography takes us right to the end of Ueshiba's life, it stops after a different point has been established, namely that the most central fact about Aikido was Morihei Ueshiba's establishment of Aikikai, run by his successors, his unbroken line for eternity. Less emphasized is the situation in late Tokugawa Japan that gave rise to Deguchi or Omoto-kyo and to many other "new" religions as well as their common features".*

But, further on and in the same article, Peter tells us that "it is debatable whether Ueshiba's embrace of Omoto—in spite of the Mongolian expedition—led to any political activity on his part whatsoever. Of course, the mere fact of Ueshiba's participation in this expedition might be taken as evidence of direct and active political involvement, but I think this would need to be corroborated by other evidence". Or "... I think that a protest against a new fisheries law and the protest organized by Kumagusu Minakata against shrine consolidation (from 1906 until 1921) were, in fact, the only popular protest movements that Morihei Ueshiba was ever involved in. When he met Onisaburo Deguchi and susequently joined Omoto, opportunities for protest were right there in front of him, but he appears never to have joined in Deguchi's overtly political activities. Ueshiba viewed his mission in life in much more personal terms, appropriate only to himself. And, though he might well have retired to Iwama as a result of his unease with Japanese military policies, this unease remained just that—an unease—and it never affected his lofty vision of the Emperor system and his role in its realization. To judge from Takemusu Aiki discourse, Ueshiba conceived this vision in the same cosmic but ethnocentric terms as Deguchi. (...) Daito-ryu, Aiki-budo and Aikido were never really involved in any pre-war popular protest movements, and the same is true of post-war Aikido in Japan. Aikido is regarded as a pillar of Japanese society and is in no sense "counter-cultural" in the revolutionary sense of the word. In some respects, this is different from the impression I have of some Aikido groups abroad. For example, a group like Aiki Extensions is actively involved in using principles it believes intrinsic to Aikido to achieve major political changes—rather like an Aikido Greenpeace. In Japan, Aikido is nowhere to be seen in popular movements dealing with world issues, and all martial arts are conspicuous by their silence with regard to peace issues here in Hiroshima..." (Omoto and the National Essence, Peter Goldsbury, Aikiweb - Transmission- Inheritance-Emulation #7).

For those who are interested and have the time, I highly recommend an extraordinary series of long articles by **Peter Goldsbury** on the history of contemporary Aikido and, above all, what is—in my opinion—the real biography of Ueshiba Morihei that you can still find online at www.aikiweb.com/columns Transmission, Inheritance, Emulation (Chapters #1-28).

AIKIBUDO, AIKI-JUJUTSU OR AIKIDO?

- This whole question is important, but there are others that are perhaps more interesting. For example, how did we manage to go from the idea of Takeda Sokaku's Daito-ryu Aiki-jujutsu—very technical and still very much borrowed from the old bellicose, cultural time of the samurai—to the idea Aikibudo*. Or, for that matter, to the idea of Aikido—an educative art of "peace" and hence the "Bu-do of love without competition"?

*Aikibudo, as represented by Master Alain Floquet in France, and—at least for its Aiki-budo part—is more or less a direct product of Tokikimune Takeda's dojo at Abashiri (Hokkaido). Aikibudo is the Tokimune version of his father Takeda Sokaku's Daito-ryu mixed with the Hono-ha-Ryu** sword school which, after the war, wanted to transform Aiki-jujutsu of Daito-ryu into Budo (Art of War transformed to Art of Peace). That is to say, to keep the Daito-ryu base but put it within reach of modern times: echoes of Shoden? N.B. Floquet in his school retains part of this inheritance, which he composed based on the knowledge of other schools ...).

** "You are not doing Aiki-Budo unless you practice both sword and jujutsu, that is to say, unless you practice both Daito-ryu and Ono-ha Itto-ryu" (Aiki News #88 – Interview with Tokimune Takeda - 1991)

The idea was both avant-garde and very determined. But first of all, to try to understand all this—and before attempting to grasp a kind of photograph of Aikido's internal philosophy, a subject dealt with later on in this book—it maybe time to ask yourself, "What was—and what is—Daito-ryu Aiki-jujutsu in relation to what we know today about Aikido"?

However, we will remain cautious in our remarks since the term "Aiki-jujutsu" itself has now become slightly taboo in the world of Aikido where it often provokes an ill-natured frown on the brow of this microworld's elite. The reverse is also true since Aiki-jujutsu sensei complain about Aikido and clearly separate it from their own practice with a rather denigrating air saying, "It is only a vague copy."

It is my hope that all those who see themselves as more sectarian than I am, will forgive me so that both sides of the aisle—in the interest of information and research—will defy this "mutually agreed" prohibition as we forge on.

DAITO-RYU AIKI-JUJUTSU - When you first take a look at it, Daito-ryu Aiki-jujutsu seems quite clear and understandable. In comparison with Aikido, there doesn't seem to be many external differences, except that the Aiki-jujutsu practitioner moves much less and seems much less aesthetic. Again, at first sight, this art does not appear spectacular or "demonstratively effective" either, and besides, unlike with Aikido masters, the "big boys" are not

necessarily there in force. Remember that, while it seems Takeda Sokaku had arms "hard as the root of a tree"—Japanese fencing and his ambidexterity caused or necessitated this—he was only one metre fifty high and, although hypertonic, was not especially muscular in the body building sense of the word. Similarly, today, women's Aiki-jujutsu is well developed compared to Aikido where, proportional to the number of practitioners, women are almost non-existent. And here I'm not talking about Aikido practiced by forty-kilogram women, which is, in my opinion, a nameless aberration and absolute technical nonsense. Except for a brilliant nagare, but here—and more's the pity—we are getting into the realm of the almost never seen!

The descendants of the (formal) Oshiki-uchi practitioners are not very demonstrative: if they are concerned about the right attitude and the right detail, if shisei (posture) or angles of work are important for them, they don't seem to care too much about their visible elegance.

Aikido-jujutsu is even devoid of the "sensational", "irresistibly superb", or "aesthetically convincing" side seen in today's Aikido, but I won't let myself get sidetracked here on that issue. In any event, should any further evidence of all this be needed, one of the favourite sayings of my own school (Daito-ryu Aiki-jujutsu Shikoku Hombu Dojo) is: "A movement is executed on the surface of a single tatami, and a single second is the ideal time needed" or, in Japanese:

"AIKI-WAZA WA: ICHI-JO, ICHI-BYO"

So, although Daito-ryu is, in fact, quite refined in its execution points and its technical depth, unlike Aikido, it appears "obsolete" and almost clumsy from a visual perspective.

On the other hand, if you want to actually practice it, that's another matter altogether, and improvisation just doesn't cut it—even for seasoned Aikido practitioners. As for being subjected to it, one is often left completely nonplussed by so many things, without really understanding what's happening within the movements. So much so that their details remain for the most part indecipherable and mysterious to the uninitiated—even to undergo them, and even to want to decipher and reinvent them.

This original, uncompromising, sober and utilitarian martial art—and I refer here to Takeda Sokaku's Daito-ryu Aiki-jujutsu—consists, whatever the attack, in controlling—step by step, point by point—each potentiality, positioning and physiological dynamic of an adversary's weakness. And this, so as to "open" them up or to "penetrate" them in order to immobilize or prevent potential for a strong offensive and the freedom that would allow it.

For this purpose, "sticky, dissipating, embracing, or penetrating" contacts are used at the articular level (internal surfaces), vital points, and body or dynamic levels, allowing very refined control connections. And, above all, "links to the adversary" which—by their very nature—incapacitate him throughout a movement.

So we say in Daito-ryu: "To touch one's opponent is to defeat him". And actually, it really works!

In this way, Daito-ryu nomenclature contains hundreds and hundreds of different movements, each of which, uniquely and in its own right, corresponds to attacks that are also duly listed. Or to natural forms of struggle (anatomical), even to the point of them corresponding to the particular morphology of an adversary.

Many movements were abandoned or lost during its history leading up to the defeat of the user clans in 1868. But still today there are thousands of movements for unarmed combat alone, not to mention for other specialties involving weapons such as spears, long and short sabre, knife, war fan and jet weapons. As well as for policing and law enforcement techniques, tying up prisoners, defense in close quarters, and both one-handed and armed combat. These movements from Takeda Sokaku's teaching are classified by thematic groups, and are sometimes different if the attacks come from the right or the left—or if they are carried out while standing or on the knees. Also, they are adapted to deal with combinations of attacks—for example, immobilizing attacks that are pull-push—or attacks that are simple or combined, armed or unarmed, and so on.

If you think about it, that means it would take at least eighteen years non-stop—usually they say twenty in the business—to only study the 2884 listed unarmed techniques. And this, diligently learning three different techniques a week in an efficient manner. Personally, I'd be happy if someone actually named all these techniques for me. Anyway, don't hold your breath on that one!

And even then, you still have the choice. While some of these schools remain faithful to Takeda Sokaku's teaching and include all techniques*, this is not always the case. For example, even the **Takuma-Kai** school (formed by Hisa Takuma, a direct student of Takeda) doesn't necessarily include the old techniques in armour or, more generally, those of weaponry. In other words, though based on the teaching of Takeda Sokaku, each school has more or less specialized in this or that side of Daito-ryu.

So, now that the reader knows a little more about Daito-ryu, let's move forward and take a look at how the founders of Aikido managed to distill their art from the plethora of Daito-ryu Aiki-jujutsu techniques.

One such school was that of Takeda Tokimune (1915-1992), son of Sokaku Takeda. He was deeply involved in his father's Daito-ryu Aikijujutsu, changed its name to Daito-ryu-Aikibudo in 1954, and mainly taught it in northern Japan (in Abashiri, Hokkaido). He settled at the end of his life in Tokyo. On his death, his successor in 1992 was his brother, Takeda Munemitsu, who took up the flame in the Japanese capital, before "the advent" of Kondo Sensei who "recaptured" the territory.

FROM AIKI-JUJUTSU TO AIKIDO -

The self-appointed custodians of Aikido came up with several notions to distinguish it from all the complications of Daito-ryu. One of them was the idea of selecting some of the most significant movements of the Aiki-jujutsu repertoire, and most of the time, it was the title or lead items in progressive-development lists of Daito-ryu movements. Hence the names of "movement groups" were transformed into de facto unique "principles" or "teachings". At this point, readers must be saying to themselves, "Hold on a moment. That's a bit strange, isn't it…"!

Some examples of rather bizarre approach to movement development and naming are given below.

Daito-Ryu Ikajo 一ケ条. This includes, among others, the so-called "Ippon-dori" 一本浦 movements, which are the first movements in Tokimune Takeda's list (son of Takeda Sokaku) who founded the current nomenclature of today's Daito-ryu. The term "Ippon-dori*" (under the list entitled "Ikajo") is a term that actually means "taking (tori, torraeru, tsukamaru) of the bar (ippon)". These Daito-ryu Aiki-jujutsu movements—called "manipulation of the bar of the arm" because, in principle, an attacking arm or one in danger stiffens—became the unique movement of … "Ikyo" in Aikido. The ancient term "Ikajo" therefore, originally meant the list of Daito-ryu's "first thirty techniques" (**plural**). Now "Ikajo" 一ケ条 was transformed into Aikido's "**Ikkyo**" 一教 or, in other words, **the** "first teaching" (**singular**) with, however, the peculiarity of imposing an "omote" form (positive) and a negative form, "ura";

*"Sokaku's swordsmanship came from the traditional Ono-ha Itto-ryu sabre school. The first short sword technique in this art is the same as the first technique in Daito-ryu (Ippon-dori) where you pin your opponent then thrust at and cut him. This technique was used only during the civil war era but Sokaku taught it as the most important technique".
(Interview with Tokimune Takeda (Aiki News #37)

Daito-ryu Nikajo 二ケ条: the list **of** the "second thirty techniques", transformed now into Aikodo's **Nikyo** 二教 or **the** "second teaching";

Daito-ryu Sankajo 三ケ条: the list of the "third thirty techniques", transformed now into Aikido's **Sankyo** 三教 or **the** "third teaching".

The list goes on until we reach the famous Aikido G**okyo** 五教 immobilisation technique. This is the head, if we can use the word, of the fifth column and which resumes the principles of the four other previous basics. But this time with work on the thumb, something few practitioners know about anyway!

In this way, they—by this, I mean those famous custodians of Aikido—were able to see a common denominator between the diverse variations of such and such a series of Daito-ryu movements. And this, so they could determine movements that would later—and in all seriousness—be said to be "generic " in Aikido. As for all martial arts, these basic movements were called "**Kihon**" 基本.

Moreover, we will later find some of these variations in what were improperly called Aikido "applications" or worse still, "forgotten movements". While this approach would make History smile broadly, it will make Daito-ryu practitioners laugh until they cry. But then again, it's an approach which has apparently never alerted or bothered any of our Aikido "grand masters". Nonetheless, there are profound reasons for these choices but, since it would take too long to explain, I will not broach the subject at this point. But you should know that, as is always the case in Japan, nothing was done randomly. Quite the opposite, in fact!

After extracting these common denominators, they then naturally tried to learn how to carry out each of the resulting selected techniques, but this time in a simplified way and with the greatest number of possible attacks. In this way, the repertoire was (and became) a very simple but rather artificial base of about twenty major movements multiplied by about thirty predetermined attacks. It is this suite or collection that formed post-war Aikido and which—through a kind of hardening or coagulation and constant "purification" blindly continued up until today—forms contemporary Aikido.

THE TRUTH WITHIN THE FACTS -

In an effort to truly understand what was changed regarding Aiki-jujutsu when Aikido was formulated, one has to take into account deliberate decisions that were made at the highest level. The three main ones are as follows:

- All movements that are potentially dangerous when executed, to be dropped one by one;

- All movements that are complicated or difficult to execute, to be dropped one by one*;

- All movements revealing "too many" Aiki secrets to be dropped one by one.

Ikkyo in Aikido being the exception that confirms the rule (in terms of its ease of execution, that is) since Aikidoka have only kept in their repertoire the difficult version where one starts on the elbow instead of extending the partner's arm. Moreover, as no one knows how this technique was done in the old days—or why—today everyone, in Ikkyo, simply pushes on the partner. Which, of course, doesn't work very well since everyone stumbles on the impossibility of "push the wall". And yet no one—or almost no one—asks any questions—questions a simple rabbit would ask when crossing the road. I think, moreover, that O Sensei had deliberately favoured this form, because it seemed more logical, and especially does not reveal the secret of this fundamental Aiki technique. This is why Ueshiba Morihei said at the end of his life, "Ikkyo needs to be studied all one's life". You astonish me, Georges, because using this particular version, Ikkyo becomes impossible to execute without its key of operation. And, on the other hand, from what one can see here and there, remains impossible to reinvent. And this, in spite of what I must admit is the indisputable geo-find-all inventive faculty of many current masters!.

This is, by the way, the same cherry-picking approach that Jigoro Kano used to "invent" Judo from the thousands of diffused Ju-jitsu techniques.

And it is these few "surviving" movements of Daito-ryu Aiki-jujutsu—themselves simplified or reconstituted in the same simplification-normalization perspective—which have become what we call "**the basics or fundamentals**" of Aikido.

On the other hand, apart from its classification by theme*—Daito-ryu Aiki-jutsu had a very special learning progression, very different from what it has become in today's Aikido. It must be said that Takeda Sokaku always showed his students his techniques only once. He did not go back over them on another day since, having already shown them to his students, he considered that they were learned, understood and assimilated. And it wasn't permissible to ask questions without provoking his anger. It was then the students duty to instantly remember and capture the subtleties and essence of what Sokaku was showing them. And the originality of this "method" obviously required immense, pragmatic, and concentrated attention.

While classification of these techniques was done later by various schools, we find the same types of "serial" progression there, though more or less simplified. Numerous subdivisions of levels and of teaching continue to exist, no doubt recapitulating the main outlines of Sokaku's very individual teaching method. And this method included the habit of teaching what was attainable for each individual student, which explains why he mainly taught Aiki techniques to Ueshiba who had a slight body structure.

* The list in Sokaku Takeda's menkyo-kaiden had the following headings, each characterized by a certain number of duly learned and integrated

techniques: Shoden, Aiki-no-jutsu, Hiden-no-ogi, Nito-ryu Hiden, Goshinyonote , Kaishakusouden-no-koto and kaiden-no-koto.

On top of that, we must remember that the general educational foundation of Japanese teaching of the arts in general—and martial arts in particular—was the progression to knowlege through three differentiated layers of accessibility. These three pedagogic phases were called **Shoden**, **Chuden** and **Joden**, and they correspond to:

- **Kohai** or the period during which the elders of a school observed the student. This time of "non-learning"—or at least superficial learning—could, in general, last a year or even several years;

- **Shoden.** This is the "traditional departure" or start of teaching, and the version open to the "public at large". The teaching was done in the form of kata with kata being the indexed form, a kind of dictionary of the art or shell of learning for beginner or intermediate students. And it was this shoden which led to **shu** or the embrace of the contents of the kata—of the form—by imitating the master. This was often done with total obedience or, in other words, personal quasi-servitude;

- **Chuden**, the tradition internal to the school. This is the mastery or conceptual teaching for advanced students already familiar with shoden. It involves the applications (bunkai) of the kata to arrive at **Ha,** the know-how to diverge from the kata. Here one usually goes from the title of "Sensei" to that of "Shidoshi";

- **Joden** or **Okuden**. This is the deep, secret tradition of a school, and it represents the teaching of the essence of a school (ryu) for students finally reaching a higher level of mastery. Hence the title of shidoshi. It is this joden or okuden which leads to **Ri**, the rejection of the Kata while keeping its clarity or creative freedom within a defined practice. In other words, the content of a kata—its direction or sense if you prefer—can be fully and freely expressed within its structure, a structure which, on the other hand, is itself defined and fixed. **Okuden** here means the secret character of this technical side of the art.

Besides what I've just said—or rather in a technical superimposition on the pedagogical progression*—the general progression in, for example, Daito-ryu remains more or less sequential as outlined below.

* *Westerners still believe Japan does not know or even ignores pedagogy, and I think this is a gross and conceited error of judgment. The Japanese simply have a pedagogy which is completely baffling for us because it's nearly based on the long term and, I find, imbued with an opportunistic pragmatism utilitarian to Buddhist conditioning. As well as being very Confucian..*

Jujutsu: First of all, we have to learn the techniques of jujutsu, that is to say, the primary techniques of combat, rustic techniques of warlike efficiency, and pragmatic techniques of self defense. This must be done with vigour and pragmatism—succeed or not—and without asking too much about the finesse of the techniques. It really doesn't matter if it's really correct or not, they must just work!

Aiki-jujutsu: Students who've proven themselves at this first level—considered to be very basic—can begin, to put it very simply, to add "Aiki" into the jujutsu techniques. In other words, to tackle Aiki techniques at the level of anatomical implications of the partner-aggressor in a stabilized starting position. This leads to the question of just how to "pass" the **jujutsu** techniques "inside" the body (or the movement) of a strong, or solid partner. And this, without any unforseen rupture or anatomical opposition that inevitably lead to resistance, blockages, counter-attacks or "counters". Shiro Omiya, a pupil of Master Tsuruyama—himself a former pupil of Takuma Hisa—talks in this way about "Martial Yoga". It's a question of "Ki-no-**awase**"—the concord of the Ki—or the "Ki-no-**musubi**"—knotting up or blending of one's Ki with that of the partner—through very refined technical principles.

These technical principles include principles of pulleys (in the plural here), cuts inside cuts, infiltration of forces, special use of the hands and fingers, uses of the structural framework of the body, articular entries, imbalances, putting out of allignment, vertical or horizontal dissipations, aspirations or contractions, and so on.

Aiki-no-jutsu: Finally—and reserved for the best of the students—came the learning of "Aiki of Action", often this time at the heart of an aggressive movement by the opponent. So it's frequently a question of a kind of "gearing-down Aiki", sometimes operating "in anticipation". In this way, one can work with the minimum of effort—in an attack coming to its finality, in the process of arriving (sen-no-sen), or even by provoking it (hi-kake)—to then "lead" the partner to be at one's feet. This facet of the art in fluid action—later called "**Ki-no-nagare**" (flow of Ki) or, as French Eric Grousillat nicely defines it: "… in all logic, we don't allow the partner to fully implement his attack" (Budoshugyosha, "The base of bases"). Now this ki-no-nagare included most of the high-level Daito-ryu movements, such as kakete (架けて) meaning "erect" (a bridge), "suspend between two points", "build", "support " and so on.

Apart from its extremely technical aspect, it also brought into play manipulation faculties, even sometimes ones with an occult or spiritual character such as lures and "**ma**" work—management of distance between partners—points or directions of weaknesses or reflexes, and psychological manipulation. Or even surprising principles of physical manipulation of forces, spiritual mudra ritual gestures of Indian religious origin that, it must be remembered, we also find in Shinto and, of course, in esoteric Buddhism, Ki-Ai, and so on.

Without overextending ourselves here, let's not forget that the three ancient stages of the educational progression in Daito-ryu, Aikido's ancestor, can be summarized as follows:

- **Ju-jutsu:** the raw **Ki**, the energy, the brute force **Awase** which allows us to gauge the prime motivation of a practitioner;

- **Aiki-jujutsu:** the Ki-no-**awase** which allows us to gauge the technical finesse of a practitioner;

- **Aiki-no-jutsu**: the Ki-no-**nagare-awase** which allows us to gauge a practitioner's applicative understanding.

In fact, we really must remember them since they still represent—although often even in caricatured ways—Aikido's principal trends as it is represented in the world today. In fact, it's very often desire to know which one is correct—or more correct than the others—that causes the inter-organization struggles to continue on, without giving their completeness even a moment's thought. And paradoxically, it is these three (Daito-ryu) categories that provide a fairly good representation of the positive levels of practice among Aikido practitioners or, to be nice, let's say their "good sides". And this, as we have just seen, without Aikido teachers themselves—irrespective of their ranking—even suspecting this is the case.

You will perhaps also hear discussions about the variety of ways one can execute movements during a workout. Let's talk about it very briefly here. They are as follows:

- **Ko-tai** (solid work): kihon or basics (steady, solid start);

- **Ju-tai** (supple or flexible work): ki no nagare, that is work on the dynamic of a partner's movement without a pronounced stop or "break";

- **Ryu-tai** (supple body);

- **Ki-tai** where one guides the partner as soon as his intention appears. This is Takemusu Aikido, an advanced technique in which the partner is hardly touched at all, and it represents the ultimate stage of absolute anticipation.

Others still exist—in fact, as many as one wants—in the sense that they are only pedagogical inventions which often depend on the nomenclature of a particular school, a sensei, a style, or a dojo. But, diversity aside, we must now continue on with our historical progression to Aikido.

THE "FOUNDATION" OF THE CURRENT AIKIDO

- It is Aiki-no-jutsu, the ultimate stage in the study of Aiki comprising anticipation (work "in time") and reductive practice (work with a minimum of effort), that was more or less chosen—paradoxically as it turns out—to become the common yardstick by which Aikido is measured today. In other words, Aiki's expression of "Do".

Now this is quite understandable because it's the one which, as we have seen, Takeda Sokaku primarily taught to Morihei Ueshiba. It was also the one that seemed the simplest to convey, the most "demonstrative" and, above all, the most surprising.

Moreover, because it meant working almost always in motion and—in accord with the Aiki concept—on principles of displacement, withdrawal, pivot, fading, training and partner imbalance. Yamaguchi Sensei (1924-1996) was the master who technically developed this form of practice—called "in nagare"—to its highest point, not leaving out of his practice the original Aiki basics of Aiki-jujutsu. But who of those who later relied on him or used his name, noticed? I have to admit that I myself only became aware of it when I studied Daito-ryu. And, over the years, it was a great surprise for me to discover that the fundamentals of Yamaguchi Sensei's Aikido, though not noticeable at first, were—in his own subtle and agile way, of course—very closely corrrelated with the fundamentals of Daito-ryu.

Now these new modes or compositions of martial art (Aikido, for one) were believed to be already well understood—erroneously, in fact—in other martial arts circles like, for example, those of judo or its ju-jitsu ancestors. And this led to twenty different ryu (schools) being represented, for example, in France today.

And so it's hardly a coincidence that, at the start of its introduction, the pioneers of Aikido in France or in the West came from the world of judo. Truth was that this sport—in full expansive mode at the time—did vaguely recognize Aikido as a parent art. In fact, as an art which was even a little more exotic than ju-jitsu* itself.

It's important to realize that the ju-jitsu were mainly of (or sometimes recovered from) historical plebeian origins in Japan. Above all, it was practiced by those who didn't wear swords at their belts, for example, peasants, merchants, doctors, craftsmen, members of the police, etc. On the other hand, from its origin, Aiki-jujutsu was always a warrior art reserved for samurai casts and characters of high social standing such as nobility. As we have already seen, it was a fighting art that had been developed for high-ranking inhabitants of castles, and first of all, taking into account the way of life in a castle and an attack inside it. This, for example, is the reason for the very important continuation of kneeling work in Aikido (shikko) which simply doesn't exist in other martial arts, and no more so than in Ju-jitsu, for example. Aiki-jujutsu was therefore an exclusively noble art. Moreover, and according to Minoru Mochizuki's recollections, the fees for Morihei Ueshiba's twentieth-century dojo, the Kobukan, were in line with this sense of social elitism. "The initial salary for a university graduate at that time was thirty-five yen—a kind of minimum wage reference in Japan—and, while the monthly fee at the Ueshiba dojo around 1933 was thirty yen, it was three yen at Jigoro Kano's judo dojo, the Kodokan. There were only rich students at the Kobukan dojo since those who were poor simply could not come. Ueshiba Sensei was not poor, of course, and he did not lead a rich life, but he had to feed people like us, the uchi-deshi." (Aiki News #72 (September 1986) translated by Damien Gauthier. But even the world of Western judo was unaware of it then. Just like the Aikido federations even today. Federations that could have taken a different «way» and used this extraordinary "cultural lever" to elevate Aikido to the rank of search for the "nobility of self" instead of lowering it towards the brutish dictum of the "stronger or better than my neighbour".

Putting aside the fact Aikido's official French introduction was the work of Minoru Mochizuki—he came to teach judo in 1951—and even that André Noquet* was a judo teacher, the initial understanding of it was flawed. For European judoka in the fifties, Ueshiba's Aikido was a little bit like a kind of "dynamic super-ju-jitsu" they had discovered without understanding its unique technical, cultural or historical aspects.

*André Noquet (1914-1999). We shouldn't underestimate the quite enormous influence of André Noquet in the synthetic development of today's "modern" Aikido (post-war). André Noquet, WWII resistence member and holder of the Croix de Guerre, was promoted by Aikikai to 8th Dan in 1985 and made Knight of the Legion of honour in France in April 1994. A very Catholic man, a judoka and an athlete emeritus, he was also in Los Angeles—after leaving Japan—as an instructor of self-defense for the California police. Well placed at Western embassies in Japan—he was responsible at the time for a Franco-Japanese cultural mission—he was invited to Japan and entered Aikikai as an uchi-deshi in 1955 alongside the founder. He was a foreigner but managed to gain Kisshomaru Ueshiba's family confidence and ear in the development of post-war Aikido. I personally think the whole so-called "moral" side of contemporary Aikido (in the Christian or Jesuitic sense of the term) along with the development of the ideas of universal peace in Aikido—albeit stemming from the Gnostic thought of Ueshiba Morihei—come largely from his influence with Morihei, Kisshomaru, and the Aikikai Sensei at that great time. And it must be said, at the cost of many revisionisms: it is, for example, a Western interpretation or translation more understandable for us Westerners. An example of this is the completely vague notion or translation—a kind of master key—of the word "harmony", or again, another revisionism of the same kind "Zen and Aikido are one". Not to mention the global influence of judo on Aikido up until today, and so on. See his biography on Guillaume Erard's site:
https://www.guillaumeerard.com/aikido/articles/biography-of-andre-nocquet-the-first-foreign-student-of-morihei-ueshiba*

The use of local logistic training structures—rooms with tatami mats, clubs or existing associations—finally explain the reason for the relative craze for superimposing Aikido onto judo... a craze that, in my opinion, turned out to be a great opportunity. However, one of the great misfortunes of this Western import of Aikido was the overconfusion of styles it imposed. Confusion that became ... ouch, a reference!

On the other hand—and here we are about to discover an extraordianary link between judo and Aikido—it should be noted that one of the greatest pioneers of modern judo was Shida Shiro (1866-1922), better known as "The Cat of Kodokan". In fact, Jigoro Kano in Japan offered him directorship of the Kodokan, but he refused. Of course, it must be realized that Shido Shiro was not only Tanomo Chikamasa's adopted son from the age of nine, but also one of two former students before he became his son-in-law by marrying his daughter. And, as we have seen, another of Tanamo's students was Takeda Sokaku who, at the beginning of their relationship, was his bodyguard. Shida Shiro's favourite judo technique—his "special"—was the famous Yama-arashi (mountain storm), a kind of shoulder projection similar to the start of a shiho-nage (360° direction throw) crossed up and down. At a time when one wanted to demonstrate the superiority of Jigoro Kano's judo, it was this technique which made him win in his judo tournaments. And, believe it or not, it was a technique of Daito-ryu Aiki-jujutsu, in fact, a kind of juji-garami, or "kuruma-daoshi-karame-nage" which one could, in fact, qualify as being a special form of ...an Aiki-jujutsu Seio-nage! Q.E.D. or, in plain English, therein lies the proof.

TOWARDS A "MODERN" AIKIDO, BUT ONE IN SEARCH OF ITSELF! -

The "sifting" of Daito-ryu techniques hardly posed any major problems for direct students of Aikido founder, Morihei Ueshiba. The fact was that students formed more or less deeply by the Master, had **unconsciously and corporally** absorbed the necessary foundations of appearance and sensation, even without having directly learned the underlying principles of Daito-ryu. In other words, at least for themselves, they really knew how to mime Aiki's technical content. Here we are talking only about the very few Daito-ryu techniques that remained active in Aikido, and this was certainly less than fifty. In addition, many of them also practiced or had practiced Daito-ryu up to a very good level.

But afterwards, of course, a problem quickly arose since Aiki had reached its zenith as a martial art, but one without the technically efficient basics of Aiki's **jujutsu**. And the result was what one would expect: the movements no longer worked well at all. So it became necessary—especially for the successors of Kisshomaru Ueshiba, for example—to quickly **reinvent conditions of success** for the movements. In reality, they reinvented nothing, but rather created conditions under which the movements worked—or at least worked better. This was needed to find a potentially viable technical base for this upscale martial art which had, in reality, become something of "a hollow pyramid", "a pyramid built on sand".

The fact is Aikido had become a kind of "placebo" martial art which—admittedly "fascinating"—was one without any of its original technical warranty. Blatant proof of this can be seen in the current official Aikido way of doing ikkyo or nikyo techniques.This is, in many respects, often the opposite or a great confused mixture compared, for example, to the numerous (thirty different approaches) of ikkyo in Daito-Ryu. And, above all, the problem is germane to the original basic principle for this kind of movement where, for example, compared to Daito-ryu, one can count about twenty important principles on a movement like ikkyo in Aikido. Not to mention what guided the inventive formulation of the five bases of "ikkyo up to gokyo", a formulation which formerly meant they they could be done according to the level of the practitioners, their skills, their morphology, and their circumstances. Hence the birth of "parrot-fashion explanations", "cyclone" movements, and the big "Magic-Circus". As well as the so-called "kind" masters exhibiting a false calm, or the sudden appearance of personal "styles" of Aikido—all of which were, for those conversant with the art's origins, often completely out of sync with any reality of its historic direction or meaning. And there's more: styles that, having lost touch with their original benchmarks, were sometimes completely psychotic or neurotic, imbued with immense pride and no lesser ignorance, and often of a quasi self-taught and hallucinatory nature.

It is for this reason that, over time, Aikido—on the tatami mats that is—most often became a vague form of dressage during which the master became the tamer of his students who, little by little, become Pavlovian animals. And this form of Aikido—one that should never be questioned—was graced or justified with the epithet "It always works". On top of that, it became a trial of strength or a game played by dupes characterized by the idiom, "now you see me, now you don't!" And, it has to be said that the lack of competition didn't sort out the problem either, in the sense of reality itself at any rate.

In any event, the result of these two bad habits, was the indirect teaching of truckloads of mania to win as well as strange obsessions—peculiar to aikidoka—with this or that allegiance. In Japanese, this is called "**kusei**" which means tic, mania, taste, habit, a kind of failed plaster casting or "crease or wrinkle" in the practice. An example of this phenomenon can be seen in the mania for the "touch" during atemi movements, for example, for uke. And this, without even knowing or ever having tested whether there is a convincing or conclusive result from this or that technique or part of technique. In this regard, the practice of karate doesn't change anything. Other examples are: rigid bodies or bodies out of sync with their basic reflexes, on seizures, for example (Ah: morote-dori!); stereotyped anticipations of movements; unrealistic attacks or those having completely lost their meaning; and ukemi by collusion or agreement. And so many more, I simply give up.

Anyway, as we all know perfectly well—without knowing quite why—the movements had to "pass", had to be accepted! And so we quickly arrived at styles characterized by expressions like "community of acrobats specialized in organized gliding". Or

"Caterpillar why are you scared"? And, conversely, that of "liar's poker with "O.K. You've seen nothing. You loose". Or obviously, a mixture of all three at the same time. This brought further disorder, an indescribable confusion to the art and endless quarrels over what to do or finally what not to do in Aikido.

In short, it was right back to the "sporting-macho-antagonists" image common for most martial arts. After a thousand years of history and improvement, in less than forty years, Aiki had regressed like never before. It became exactly like the theatre of a vast and noisy cattle market where the truth was no longer proveable or, for that matter, to be found. And where everything was worth something, meaning, in general, nothing was worth anything. So, considering the cacophonous state of affairs, the question that comes to mind is quite simply, why ?

WHY THIS TURNING POINT?

- It was believed that the adoption of a sporting and educational direction to popularize this art—Kano's model in judo—would solve the martiality problem of "Aikido" techniques in its mass teaching. Why? Because speed, surprise, joint pain (local and unbearable), as well as brute force would serve to replace **ancestral anatomical and dynamic adequacy**, and thus the true "Aiki" of the movements. This infernal trio of "speed, surprise and pain" also replaced the key points and the terminal points of the movements*.

** Here I am talking about the main immobilisations and, for example, what was then called the **"Kime"** of a technique, namely "the decisive epilogue" aimed at completely nullifying the forces and freedom of action*

of the aggressor. These immobilizations are most often associated with conclusive Atemi either putting the aggressor into a position of giving up (abandonment) or directly out of action.

One mustn't believe, in fact, that Aiki-jujutsu was only a philosophical pleasure game or some kind of anecdotal martial practice. I can assure you that, having personally discovered many many examples, it was at the bottom of absolutely dreadful techniques that were really disabling or even extremely cruel and destructive to a point probably few people can even imagine nowadays. There was, in fact, a spectrum of techniques, and its two extremities were: police-type **neutralization techniques**; **warfare techniques** which, by their very nature, were both sudden and lethal.

These techniques were so much part of the art's DNA that, even in Daito-ryu nowadays, almost no master knows or even teaches these second types of old deadly forms as—even in training—they can be disabling. The risk is simply too great! In this respect, perhaps it's not so bad since, if it doesn't lose its essence, of course, it means Daito-ryu can become "civilized".

But let's return to Aikido as well as Morihei Ueshiba's esoteric philosophy which, while very interesting in itself, has more or less been abandoned by the Japanese themselves. The basic basic lack of "Aiki" foundation in Aiki-do continued to spread the malaise, namely that of the martial legitimacy and originality of this new art faced with the relentless development of other very well established martial arts.

Because, in the end, Aikido-ka scarcely managed to do as well as the others did—and that with a flabby pacifism which was entirely suspect at the time. The fact is it's simply not enough to say "no rivalry, no competition" for both rivalry and competition to disappear. It would, in fact, have needed courage and intelligence to take on this decision, not to mention the experience or possibly the cultural and "intellectual" capacity as well. And that, one suspects, was simply not there in the right place or at the right time.

AIKIDO FORMATION AND THE NATURE OF AIKI IN DAITO-RYU-

An extensive comparative study of Daito-ryu and of the Aikido techniques over many years has led me to a startling conclusion. As a result of examining their specificities, their similarities, and their differences, I am of the opinion that the official registration of the name "Ai-ki-do" with the Ministry of Health and Welfare, made for a huge confusion of meaning of the term Aiki (合気). And more than likely, in its translation into other languages, principally French and English.

The historical meaning of Aiki*—the meaning in Daito-ryu—was (and is) "The energy of union" or the "will (the key word here) to impose a unification of forces to create zero, where zero is equivalent to Ai (合) or the perfect encasement of the forces". In other words, **the will—meaning I want—to encase together or nest the forces to my benefit**.

But from 1942—coincidentally the time when Aiki was being extrapolated from its Japanese context into the outside world (principally Hawai, America, and later France)—the term Aiki underwent a dramatic reversal. Certainly this was the case in France (1950s-1960s) where I believe one can possibly see the "footprint" of André Noquet, the famous French judoka-cum-aikidoka who, to put it in a fun way, "surfed beautifully—and as a good catholic—on a Hawaiian wave".

The change was that, in Aikido, the term Aiki (合気) became "The union of energies". This infers that "the energies (key word and plural in this case) must be put together—Ai (合 means to fit together)—to create "my" desired form of harmony". In other words, **the union of the forces gives me an ideal assembling, encasement or nesting**.

* *The general vocabulary of Aikido's history includes two very messy terms—what an Englishman might call "awful slip-ups"—that have remained technically calamitous since 1942: they are **"Harmony"** and **"Union of energies"**. However, experience of Aikido on the mat makes us quickly realize these two terms work very poorly, pedagogically and technically speaking. However, I believe they just result from demagogic processes—therefore imbued with political purpose—being associated with the idea of "Do" (the way), they refer to the idea of man as a perfect social being, integrated into the order of an idealized social respectability. This is, of course, reminiscent of the famous Japanese "Ningen" (人間), a very Confucian notion of "man stuck between his rights and his duty". As for the term Aiki, it is no longer a term calling for an ontological order—as it was in the past—but rather one purely calling for a social order perceived as "superior". Superior, of course, in the sense of Japanese morality but one that, in this context, is truly close to a very "Christian" or "Jesuitical" morality—as I believe I've already talked about—and this is why they have worked so well in the West. However, so calamitous have these two terms—"Harmony" and "Union of energies"—been since 1942 that, rather than use the term "awful slip-ups", they* *might be better characterized by the words of one French humorist as being, "A Tyranosaur Rex in a porcelain shop".*

Now you may well ask yourself, just as I did, just how this reversal—one which led to a complete change in meaning—came about.

To begin an attempt at finding a reason, one has to understand that the term Aiki is written in Japanese as 合いの気 with the 合い being a form of the kanji verb Au (to put together, blend or unify), the hiragana の being "of", and the kanji 気 being force or forces. *Now it is the interpretation of the genetive (posesive) "の" that is perhaps at the root of the confusion.* If one takes the usual Japanese reverse-order way of use, Aiki would be force(s) of union or unification. Or it can mean "acting on", making Aiki "unifying or unification of forces". In addition—and to further confuse matters here—the possessive sense can be reversed (in fact, the usual Western order way of use) with Aiki's meaning coming out as "The unification of force(s)".

In any event, however it happened, during the creation of Aikido in Japan in the forties and fifties, the term Aiki certainly underwent a radical change in the meaning—a change from the historic Daito-ryu meaning to the new meaning in Aikido. This was not only a philosophical change, but also by necessity one that has profound implications for the techniques side of things. Now it is quite possible that, in Japan where subtle implications are often cleverly and skilfully perpetuated, this change might well have not been entirely accidental. And that "confusion" was not only carried over into the French and English translations, but also even possibly further accentuated.

Of course, it might appear to the uninitiated that the fact that the "I" of Daito-ryu that falls into the trap of Aikido's "Love one another" is simply a semantic or technical problem, but I believe the change or reversal of meaning is not only of paramount importance, but also vital to recognize. Whilst, as we have seen, this linguistic muddle in Japan may well have been some kind of consensual understatement—"orientable at will".

In any event, this unambiguous choice in the meaning of the word Aiki marks an almost total reversal in the values of the intention and the technical approach of the movements compared to those of historical and original Aiki. So, in this way, we witness the disappearance of movements, for example, all movements in Aiki-kake 合気掛け, Aiki-tate 合気立て, Aiki-age 合気上げ, and Aiki-sage 合気下げ simply don't exist anymore in Akido but were fundamental in Aiki-jujutsu.

But that's not all: there is another very important difference. In Daito-ryu, according to the ancient Japanese Kojiki writings, the phenomenon called Aiki is **the first thing** we put in place within a movement. On the other hand, in Aikido, Aiki is a finality or result that one seeks to obtain **at the end of a movement**. This difference between Daito-ryu and Aikido has always seemed both disturbing and uplifting for me.

To summarize then, there is a change **from Daito-ryu's** "I want to put together (encase or nest) the forces to my advantage"—very directive, martial, and voluntary right at the start of a movement **to Aikido's** "The forces this and that... that we must try to put together". So we go from **the Daito-ryu personal mode** of Aiki to **an impersonal mode** in Aikido, and this must, of course, technically influence the movements, resulting in a difference in the work done on uke or the aggressor.

In effect, in Daito-ryu, the notion of Aiki (合気) in its jujutsu (柔術)—the "I" want to seek to gather the bundles of forces at the heart of uke's body and his attack (or within his potential for attacks)—means the concretization of the following two types of interaction. Firstly, to remove oneself from any possibility of risk, danger, or counter-attack by control of the aggressor's mobility. And this, right from the beginning of his attack when we engage the original Aiki(合気) right up until his final "Maita!" (参った!) as he gives up. Secondly, and contrariwise, to put him back or assign him to a zone where the range of risk and uncontrollable danger for him is the most "disabling" possible. In this, we want to redirect a bundle or cluster of forces—often contradictory (**Ki**)—to our own advantage.

On the other hand, in Aikido and by the notion of Aiki (合気) in its Do (道), one takes into account bundles of forces within uke's aggression and his dynamics—or within his potential for attacks—to concretize the following types of interaction. To reunite all the forces involved (合気) up until there's a harmonic concordance in the movement, finally permitting a kind of double neutrality—one's own and his—and therefore "a peace" in common, incorrectly called "harmony". In this, we are not seeking our own advantage but rather an absolute balance of forces that benefits neither him nor oneself or one that benefits both parties. In other words, win-win exchanges. Such incredible exchanges existed—and still do exist—in Daito-ryu but only as one "option" among others and not as a necessity like in Aikido.

Of course, having said that, you will see that there are many documents or interviews with eminent experts*—both in Daito-ryu and Aikido—which contradict what I've just explained. I know that and, while very much aware of it, I would ask that you bear in mind that human beings generally only say, repeat or develop what they have learned, especially in the internet era where the phenomenon of blind repetition reaches its high point. I therefore offer this analysis as a general framework for discussions, and it remains for the most learned of my readers to do their own research and come to their own conclusions.

*As Peter Ustinov said, "If the world explodes, the last voice heard will be that of an expert saying that such an event is impossible."

For my part, as I have said, this whole analysis is not the end result of an intellectual process, and there were a number of factors that really bugged me and got me going on this issue.

The first was that, as I have already explained, in Daito-ryu, according to the ancient Japanese Kojiki writings, the phenomenon called Aiki is **the first thing** we put in place within a movement. On the other hand, in Aikido, Aiki is a finality or result that one seeks to obtain **at the end of a movement**.

Secondly, the fact that Aikido's "intellectual" discourse and its effects on the material world of Aikido—and here I mean in interviews, speeches and talks on the mat—are most often imbued with intrinsic contradictions. Examples are: No competition leads to fraudulent ego and veiled competition; "Harmony" leads to latent chaos poorly camouflaged by Aikido's choreographic aspects; "The union of energies" involves the permanent use of muscular strength, in the shoulders for example; the softness in Daito-ryu brings on sado-masochistic brutal relations in Aikido; and the so-called "nestings" bring on "forcing". And the combination of forces ("Ki wo gassuru" 気を合する) transforms into the infernal trio of "surprise, speed, and pain", and so on. **So we see inherent contradictions in Aikido while Daito-ryu is quite coherent.** For example, when a movement doesn't work well in Daito-ryu, unlike in Aikido, one doesn't reproach the uke for not doing what it takes for it to work. One simply blames oneself and tries to correct one's technique. This type of infantile reflection in Aikido, for me at least, have always revealed signs of martial immaturity.

And the third thing that got me going was when, one day during a course of Daito-Ryu, my Sensei, after showing me a movement I couldn't do, said something that immediately struck me, "Olivier, Aiki is to control all the uke's body supports. Aiki is to have the will (Ki:気) to gather (Ai:合) uke's body up on itself to his disadvantage". A little taken aback since it seemed the opposite to me, I then asked him to repeat himself. But he repeated the same thing—slowly and in the same order—and better still, as is appropriate, he physically demonstrated both the meaning and the relevance at the same time with several movements. He then just added, "This is the original meaning of "Aiki "(合気)."

So, in this way, we have seen the disappearance of fundamental principles, changes in the direction of intentions and purpose in the movements; and incoherence between what is said and what happens or what is done. Then there are difficulties in justifying non-sense techniques, alarming vacuity of practical analysis, pompous camouflage of choreographed gymnastics by a martial pseudo philosophy, and taboos and semantic imprecision.

The upshot is that, to solve the issues arising from the translation of Aiki's meaning into other languages, since technique generated the words—and not the opposite—we have to look to technical aspects of the movements' approach, not only at purely intellectual statements. And then, when we take this tack, the subtle reversal of the meaning of the term Aiki (合気) between "old Aiki" and "modern Aiki" suddenly becomes much clearer.

Anyhow, moving forward from the confusion for a moment, it's important that we take a look at the notion of absence of competition, the precursor of the "peace and love" aspect of Aikido.

ABSENCE OF COMPETITION - The absence of competition or rivalry in this "new" Aikido was actually quite difficult to implement—at least in our world which is essentially socially and economically dedicated to competition. It seems to me that to assert the opposite, is somewhat lacking in objectivity or reveals a very special or peculiar line of thought—possibly an epicurean type of asceticism, for example, or a discreet erasure. But, either way, it's not easy make understood. For indeed, if we imply the very opposite—"open competition"—even if we commend the inverse with a few words devoid of meaning, nobody's fooled. And it then becomes "every man for himself". Which is, of course, exactly what happened!

That is why, when faced with the "missed opportunity for relevance inherent in the post-founder's Aikido", it was quickly realized that it was necessary to completely "reinvent" or "recreate" a martial art that corresponded to something rational. In other words, to set about creating something "logical" or at least able to impress the onlookers and get them to say, "It's better than the others ... I'm going to sign up* ...".

---

* *While it's the opposite that's proof of the truth (historically speaking, of course), perhaps it's that one ought to remake history, and then the question that must be asked becomes: "Who's to gain by this"? Thus in Daito-ryu Aiki-jujutsu, when a technique is vigorously executed—even if* *it doesn't seem like it—one often hears this saying: "If a woman or a child, can't manage to execute the technique you are trying to do, because he or she cannot bring to bear these means, then that means that way of doing the technique isn't really right."*

But what can we do about it? And I say this because the bridge between the Daito-ryu Aiki-jujutsu and Aikido had been almost completely destroyed during the generation of instructors following those of the founder's direct pupils. And perhaps—this is admittedly my own assumption—as early as directly after the war when Morihei Ueshiba "broke away" from his mentor Takeda Sokaku.

Except for some rare interviews, photographs or filmed documents of Morihei Ueshiba, nobody had the whole answer or even a satisfactory answer. Above all—and this is most important to understand—nor did they have the technical keys for use of the founder's or his predecessor's ancestral secrets. Unfortunately, these things are not usually carved in stone or recorded on prints of photographic film*, but where they are, even upon very careful consultation, their meaning and details of their execution were ignored! So, having a key in hand is good, but—just the same—knowing what to do with it, how to use it, and what door of knowledge to open, is better. And a completely different approach. This becomes very obvious, for example, when one looks at the Soden photos of Sokaku Takeda taken by the Takumakai, Hisa Takuma's group. Or even when specialists and recognized masters, such as university research scientists, discuss details that allow a better understanding of these documents.

* *In this regard, the Takumakai photographic records or even those of O Sensei, the specialists consider that they represent an approach memorandum of the ancient techniques of Takeda Sokaku—nothing more and nothing of less. They are by no means "proofs" other than what they show. And so only possession of the keys of reading of these documents allows their decoding—keys of decoding that few sensei actually possess or want to deliver. So one has to be extremely careful when one uses these photographic documents to decode Aiki techniques without having a serious grounding in Aiki-jujutsu.*

Now, I was going to talk about my "uneasiness", but let's rather use the term "discomfort". I mean my discomfort with the Aikido civilization process which has endured up until now without the slightest inclination to seek out the historical truth proving the real martial value of the notion "Aiki" (reinvention not needed). The founders of Aikido aspired to—and continue to do so today—a "peaceful" warlike reality for Aikido which would be a core part of the most coherent action possible.* But it's an Aikido that is still without a philosophy, and one that, with great pride, ignores its founder's mysticism and his Aiki-jujutsu past as well as **Ki** and so on. And all that, while talking nonsense and using—just like at Catholic mass where discretion is needed because you must believe it anyway—meaningless words about Aikido's effectiveness or about "the great harmony and universal peace" everyone dreams of without ever having seen the tiniest grain of it. Amen!

* *One day, Christopher Li asked Morihei Ueshiba: (...) Is there a method for that? Or do you attack the opponent instinctively through some hidden power?"*
Mr. Ueshiba's answer replied, "There is a definite method."
"Can that method be learned by everybody?"
"It can."

(Christopher Li: "A Leap of the Spirit – Moritaka (Morihei) Ueshiba in 1932").

However, looking past the initiative of sport for the masses, the true martial quality of Aiki, the ancient and "harmonic" one—not, as we stupidly believe, the "harmonious" one—is, by its very nature, coherent. The term coherent is used here even if it (the martial quality of Aiki) isn't necessarily logical according to common criteria, genre "I do this because otherwise he might do that". This is problematic since we generally and incorrectly employ this kind of logic—always in two stages, so binary—to seek out what can only be found using the essence of another logic, often inverse and very complex. This logic is absolutely plural and indirect in that it seeks compatibility or congruence at the structural centre, the physical supports of bodies "in natural survival mode"* and the use of the body's weak points to bring it to a point of "no-action-possible" and therefore complete neutralization.

In Aiki then, to summarize, one explicitly tries to take control of the aggressor's body so as to make him assume all the risks engendered by the idea of his attack. And thus stripping his aggressivity of any freedom of action, which is very far removed from his original aim.

* **Inochi no nokori** : 命残 *or "Doing his best to survive" for Tori—the one who does Aikido—and* **Koro-shiai** *(殺試合 or " Fighting to destroy") for uke, the one who attacks. And for both, in a configuration in* **Shizentai** *(自然体) or the natural state of the body, certainly adapted to the exercise of such or such efforts, but unencumbered with unnatural involuntary reflexes. In other words, a natural body and not one with nervous tics or exhibiting psycho-physiologicoal rigidity. See also "The Life-giving Sword" and "The Death-giving Sword": Katsujin-Ken* 活人

劍 and Setsujin-Ken 殺人劍. *N.B. I will bring up these extremly important notions for the history of Aikido later in the text.*

AIKIDO: LOGICAL REFERENCES -

As we have seen in the previous section, we should be seeking out the ancient Aiki, that is to say, not the harmonious one, but the **harmonic** one. And that's not easy! Not easy at all since Aikido's "uprooting" completely removed it from its native "soil", so to speak. To a very large extent, this transfer also divested its movements of very special and specific points—its roots, in fact—which allowed for easy execution.

So we see—and I will come back to it later—that the attempts to graft this shoot onto a new theoretical, post-facto martial thought, would lead to "end the philosophy, no competition (for sure)", but conversely to "more and more training-cum-taming, more and more speed, more and more strength, and more and more... nervous tics". And, above all else, the whole song-and-dance of chronic and irreversible pain! And on top of that—I forgot to mention it—the crowning paradox of a kind of veiled competition on the mat, genre "You're not going to succeed with me!" All this produced an aberration, a "destructive" and mannerist Aikido in the short, medium and long term.

These attempts to transplant or graft this shoot onto new theoretical, post-facto martial thinking obviously didn't really manage to bring about the rediscovery of the subtleties of the original "Aiki"—except now and then. Sometimes by some masters and sometimes in a flash of genius but, it must be said, a flash often swallowed up or masked either by the habit of humdrum teaching or the hotchpotch of usually accepted practices. Or, to borrow from the philosopher Schopenhauer—so rather than an insult, it's a statement of fact—what I would call "the conspiracy of mediocrity". This is where each student in turn determines the scope of the teaching they want to encourage in their master. This approach is admittedly often not too smart and is more commonly known as "dumbing or levelling down".

On top of all that, these attempts to transplant have also not managed—for the moment at least—to unite practitioners in a sustainable way around a really viable Aikido project. And for good reason!

Since the death of the founder, the great successor masters—or would-be successors—of the art for "X" generations in the future, have chanted the recruitment song like chorus of frogs in their small pond of truth. And each one has tried—on the basis of their persona, their passion, their authoritarianism or with seductive charisma and a very personal knowledge—to attract the maximum number of blessed acolytes. It was done with a blaring, tired, old popular refrain that has nothing of Aiki left in it, bar the name. But as they say, "the truth doesn't comply with the charisma of the one who professes it".

And on that slightly dispiriting note, it's time to take a harder look at Aikido's formation and possibly question its inherent veracity.

WHERE DOES THE TRUTH OF AIKIDO LIE?

- While the question of where the truth of Aikido resides is certainly an important one, there are other related—and perhaps much more important—questions that one should be raising. Because, finally and technically, the question we should really be asking ourselves is, "When should we set about making a historic and determining halt to reflections on the "Do" or path of Aiki?". Is there, moreover, a satisfactory and legitimate historical "point of view" at which one can attempt a "freeze-frame" of a "truth about Aikido"—a truth which finally would finally define it? Today? Before the founder? After the founder? From the thirties? Starting in 1942? From 1945? 1948, the official date of creation of the Tokyo Aikikai Hombu? 1955? 1969? 1999? Maybe at the moment of his forming an *iemoto* or "authoritative" family foundation of which he was the head? On this or that "style"? On this or that master? On this or that "geography of Aikido"? On a likely future of Aikido? On the law of the greatest number? On exactly what, finally?

Historically speaking, it's quite clear Aikido's first point of origin was the discovery of the notion of "Chin-nah, Aiki, In-Yo-Do, and Taoism in the eighth century AD, followed by its subsequent recovery, reconstruction, and historical Japanese ostracism up to the present day. A process characterized by "unification through technical alliances", by personalization effects, and by specific cultural contributions, especially Taoism, but also later Neo-Confucianism, Esoteric Buddhism, Shindo-shamanism or "Shintoism", and so on. I refer to this development process once again since the synthesis factors are not only unique to Japan, but also—in my opinion—they are determining.

The second historical reference point for the synthesis is Takeda Sokaku's technical transmission of Aiki to Morihei Ueshiba and, of course, his (subsequent) universal theosophical interpretation of it. And it's Morihei Ueshiba's approach of giving a philosophical meaning to a technique of war that gives a special dimension to the idea—the very concept, in fact—of "Aikido".

The third reference point is the synthesis and technical refinement of Aiki-jujutsu's repertoire and, because of this refinement, the paradoxical abandonment of the very same repertoire which, following 1942, invented Aikido. It should be noted that 1942 was, in fact, the registration date of the name Aikido with the Japanese Ministry of Education by Minoru Hirai* on behalf of Ueshiba Morihei's **Kobukan** dojo. I would make the point here that, prior to 1942, the word Aikido didn't exist outside the vocabulary of practitioners of Daito-ryu Aiki-jujutsu.

---

* *Minoru Hirai (平井 稔 March 1903-October 1998) was a Japanese martial artist and creator of the Korindo style of Aikido. He is a very important figure in Aikido and was its main logistic promoter in the post-war period. In his youth, Minoru Hirai studied many different martial arts, including Togin-ryu, Okumura Nito-ryu, Takenouchi-ryu, Kito-ryu and Suburi-ryu. In 1938, he became a teacher of iaido and jujutsu, establishing his own dojo, the Kogado dojo in Okayama (just north of Shikoku Island). In 1938, he met Morihei Ueshiba in Okayama, who spoke to him about the **Aikibudo** technique he'd created and invited him to his Tokyo dojo. Hirai found Ueshiba's art had similarities with his own* *style of jujutsu, both being based on circular movements. He developed these ideas and decided to enter Ueshiba's Kobukan dojo (Tokyo). During the Second World War, Hirai was head of the jujutsu department of the Japanese Army's Military Police School, and helped develop new arrest techniques used by the police. In 1942, he was appointed general affairs director for the Kobukan (Ueshiba's dojo), helping him with dojo logistics. The same year he was sent as the Kobukan's representative to the Dai Nippon Butoku Kai, Japan's martial arts promotion organization. And it was in this way that he contributed to the creation of the term "**Aikido**" to designate the so-called new art of Ueshiba in the circle of Butoku Kai. A circle where he was awarded the rank of **Hanshi**.*

The fourth reference point—if one can really call it that—concerns the ongoing attempt to "fix" or graft Aikido techniques onto a martial arts project that is already completed, internationally recognized, and known by everyone as being "special and autonomous". This is what we call a "hyperonym"—a kind of umbrella organization—and it's useful to remember this word as it will be repeated later in this presentation. This fixing was attempted despite the almost total "smoothing" or technical softening of Daito-ryu techniques, not to mention their fragmentation.

And we're not done yet: it's a kind of battle over the correctness of each of the Aikido techniques that is being played out here. It's a battle taking place in the vacuum of ignorance, whose ultimate aim is to perfectly establish how this or that Aikido movement must be done. And that's it! Surely cause for the reader to laugh out loud, especially now that he or she knows a little more about the subject.

Looking at these key points, it's safe to say that Aikido is still searching for its authentic, legitimate, and peculiar martiality. Of course, it's true that this shortcoming is compensated for by a seemingly saving structural "brainwashing" embodied in enchanting and aggressive speeches—the carrot and stick approach—from the federations, clans, styles, masters, supporters and the faithful, and the various official Aikido organizations worldwide.

This "brainwashing" is almost invariably accompanied by the self-persuasion of pride—both in instructors and practitioners—largely fed by a system of transitions or rank assignments. Effectively, rather than being testimonies of a real Aiki or human technical level, they are, in fact, testimonials to the degree of subordination to a system. They are testimonies of membership and shaping in this or that "mold", and we will come back to this in the later passage on the four Aiki laws.

Much like the desire for a stripe—stars at the highest officer level—in the army, "the hope of a higher ranking" is **the** real carrot of modern martial arts in general. This is the absolute keystone of the masters' power of domination and a usually pernicious means of control—socially, economically, and in many other ways—of and in this small world. It is also a way of controlling the way the image of the art is projected onto the outside world so the neophytes, the media, etc., can finally recognize in it easily identifiable and clear merit. When we read the text below, we can see just how very far removed from the past this situation means we are.

"In those days—the Meiji era in the early twentieth century—people trained for three years after having participated in ten thousand matches with their men. They say that only then could a sworsman begin to understand how to grip a bamboo sword correctly. If they practiced a little more, they would say, "I have practiced a little..." which meant in those days that a person was a grand master. That was one of the martial artists' codewords". (Stanley A. Pranin, Aiki News # 88 – Interview with Tokimune Takeda - 1991).

I don't want to talk any more here about the cacophony of intergroup disagreements. And I do not want to say anything too much about the basic ignorance of practitioners—even often high-ranking ones—with regard to the genesis of Aikido we've seen. Or even its purely "Ai-ki" technical sense and, most of the time, the depth of its philosophy since the latter aspect remains totally inaccessible as a result of its **non-Cartesian originality**. Rather. I would like to examine the raison d'être underpinning the formation of Aikido.

WHO DID WHAT TO AIKIDO?

- It was the founder's son, Master Kisshomaru Ueshiba (1921-1999), in association with his father's direct pupils—at least those continuing to work in the family foundation—who set about the task of making Aikido an international art with a popular vocation. The word "continuing" is used here since very quickly there were divisions and—it must be said—both ejections and defections from within the ranks of the founder's very first pupils.

These defections even came from amongst the close guardians of the Ueshiba family. In Japanese, this type of family is called *iemoto* (家元), that is to say "the family root of a school", and it is a word which embodies all the continuity and power of Aikikai. There was, for example, Master Tohei Koichi (1920-2011), the chief instructor of the "**Aikikai**"* organization, and the first of Ueshiba's pupils to be allowed to officially introduce Aikido in a foreign country (USA: Hawaii in 1953).

**AIKIKAI HOMBU, the "central dojo of the Aiki association", was founded in 1948 (official name: Zaidan Hojin Aikikai-Aikido-So-Hombu) on the model of Kobu-Kai association, itself a continuation of the administrative and logistical structure of Morihei Ueshiba's dojo, the Kobukan (1930). This dojo was also called "the Dojo of Hell" for a time as the practice there was very tough. "... it was in 1948 that the Zaidan Hojin Aikikai, with its headquarters in Iwama, was approved by the Japanese Education Ministry as the postwar version of the Zaidan Hojin Kobukai" (Peter Goldsbury, Aikiweb, # Transmission-Inheritance-Emulation No. 6).*

As a point of information, we include a short chronological summary of the war and Morihei Ueshiba's wartime years*:*

"The year Morihei Ueshiba moved to Iwama saw the Battles of Coral Sea and of Midway—and the beginning of the end for the Japanese Empire—but it would have been anathema for any Japanese to express such sentiments, including O Sensei. So, perhaps we should begin this discussion with a very brief chronology of the Second World War and Aikido. with special reference to Morihei Ueshiba and the bombing of Japanese cities.

1940 August - Konoe Fumimaro proclaims 八紘一宇 *(Hakko Ichiu) meaning 'eight cords, one roof' or 'all the world under one roof'. This dictum was used by the radical Kita Ikki to justify Japan's destiny to bring peace to the world, by force, if necessary. The phrase was also used by Konoe to proclaim that the basic aim of Japan's national policy was "the establishment of world peace in conformity with the very spirit in which our nation was founded." This, as the progress of the war would show., meant many things, in fact;*

1940 August - Launch of Greater East Asia Co-Prosperity Sphere, otherwise known as "Good morning, hell" for all those who didn't bend to the Japanese will;
1940 December - O Sensei's First Series of 'Visions'
1941 Between March & October - Prince Konoe secretly sends Morihei Ueshiba to China, an event that nobody ever speaks about;
1941 December - Bombing of Pearl Harbor and, following great panic in Washington, the entry of the United States into the war;
1941 December - 大東亜戦争 : *Great Pacific War begins*
1942 April - Public demonstration to mark 10th anniversary of Manchukuo. Kisshomaru Ueshiba mentions this demonstration in his biography. This was the demonstration where Hiroshi Tada heard talk about Ueshiba's 'high-voltage' waza;
1942 April - Doolittle's B-25 raids on Tokyo, Osaka, Nagoya, and Kobe. These raids caused negligible damage but had a pronounced psychological effect in Japan since the Japanese air defenses did not shoot down a single American plane. The humiliation caused by this violation of 'sacred airspace over the Imperial capital' led to the planning of further offensive operations, all unsuccessful;
1942 May - Battle of Coral Sea;
1942 June - Battle of Midway;
1942 ? - Dai Nippon Butokukai approves 'Aikido' as the official name, resulting in exoneration from taxes;
1942 December - O Sensei's Second Series of 'Visions';
1942 'Late in the year' - Morihei Ueshiba moves to Iwama;
1943 March - Japanese retreat from Guadalcanal;
1943 April - Admiral Yamamoto, who planned Pearl Harbor, shot down;
1943 November -- Various islands in the Central Pacific overrun by the Americans;
1944 July onwards - Saipan, Tinian overrun by the Americans;
1944 July - Loss of Saipan leads to resignation of General Tojo;
1944 November - The U.S. decides to use incendiary bombs (napalm); there's no such thing as a clean war;
1945 January - Curtis LeMay takes over 21st Bomber Command;
1945 February - U.S. forces land on Iwojima;
1945 February 25 - First fire bombing of Tokyo by B-29 bombers;
1945 March 10 – three hundred and thirty-four B-29s bomb Tokyo;
1945 April - Okinawa captured by the U.S.;
1945 May - Japanese army defeated in Burma;
1945 May 23 – five hundred and twenty B-29s bomb Tokyo;
1945 May 25 – five hundred and twenty-four B-29s bomb Tokyo;
1945 May 29 – four hundred and fifty B-29s bomb Yokohama;
1945 July 8 – four hundred and ninety-seven B-29s bomb Sendai, etc.;
1945 July 12 – five hundred and six B-29s bomb Utsunomiya, etc.;

1945 July 24 – five hundred and ninety-nine B-29s bomb Osaka & Nagoya;
1945 July 28 – five hundred and sixty-two B-29s bomb Tsu;
1945 August 1 – seven hundred and sixty-six B-29s bomb Nagaoka;
In all, the B-29 bombers destroyed a total of sixty-six Japanese cities, and the bombings killed almost as many civilians as the combined atomic bombings of Hiroshima and Nagasaki. (...)
1945 August 6th and 9th – Atomic bombing of Hiroshima & Nagasaki;
1945 August 9 - Soviet Union invades Manchuria. For the record, following this invasion, Kenji Tomiki and Shigenobu Okumura were imprisoned as POWs and were not repatriated until a few years later.
1945 August 15 - Japan surrenders.
(Peter Goldsbury, Transmission, Inheritance, Emulation #10, Background)

Also, among the ranks of the defectors after the war were Osawa Kisaburo Sensei, the technical director, Shigenobu Okumura, and many others like Sadateru Arikawa, Seigo Yamaguchi, Hiroshi Tada, Shoji Nishio, Nobuyoshi Tamura and Yasuo Kobayashi. And later, Mitsugi Saotome, Masando Sasaki, Yoshimitsu Yamada, Kanai Mitsunari, Kazuo Chiba, Seiichi Sugano and several others.

These were the main "lieutenants" of the time who, with Kisshomaru Ueshiba, undertook the large-scale normalization of the art of "their father". It created an entirely new combinative panorama of movements and attacks, and a dynamic, innovative approach with its "original" technical repertoire, from then on, officially called "**Aikido**".

It is therefore mainly down to Kisshomaru Ueshiba that we owe this voluntary disconnect, this "divorce" between the Aiki-jujutsu of Daito-ryu as a whole and the new sanitized standard of Aikido. And it is also to him that we mainly owe the "eliminatory" technical choices which continued on after the death of his father—choices that were made very precisely and with incredible finesse.

But we really have to put things in context. I believe that, as far as these choices are concerned, Kisshomaru Ueshiba, who had a degree in political science, had a real vision of a political future for Aikido. Just as was done in judo, he wanted to promote several important things about Aikido:

- A "**new**" art where Aiki-jujutsu was old;

- A **simple** art finally where Aiki-jujutsu was complicated;

- A **popular** art where Aiki-jujutsu was elitist;

- An art adapted to all and **easy** to learn whereas knowledge of Aiki-jujutsu was thankless, required an excellent attentiveness and a memory no less sharp, an intellectual finesse to reach a high level, and self-sacrifice. In other words, it was very demanding to acquire, precisely what would discourage more than one would-be student;

- An art evolved into a **sport** where not many existential questions are asked anymore. And this, in sharp contrast with his father's Aiki-jujutsu which had become more and more mystical and incomprehensible for most students;

- An economically modern art with a **capitalist** vocation whereas the economic system of previous eras, as we have seen, was completely medieval and excessively expensive. It was based on the principle of patronage and creaming off of the best part of the market: the most high-priced possible for those able to pay or, put more simply, selection by money. Also, it was based on the idea of a gift—once again, a Morihei Ueshiba idea—or that of putting an exaggerated value on knowledge, for example, by establishing a monetary price for each of the new techniques taught and a system of "royalties" *ad vitam perpetuam* for the education provided (Sokaku Takeda). Moreover, this system of "renting knowledge" was certainly another of the breaking points between Sokaku Takeda and Morihei Ueshiba;

- An **international** art whereas Aïki-Jujutsu—certainly at the cultural level—was specifically Japanese in its soul, culturally medieval too, and therefore more than a little hermetic for the Westerners;

- A unique art belonging to the family. And one that was recognizable as having an **identity of its own**, whereas the Jujutsu, over the course of their history, had almost become a kind of Japanese national cultural and historical treasure in their entirety (the Ko-Budo). They shared as many trends and ryu (schools) as blades of grass in the meadow, and we're talking here about more than three thousand traditional schools in Japan.

On the death of his father, Kisshomaru, the grandson of the founder, Moriteru Ueshiba, the current Dochu or master of the way of the Aikikai world organization, placed more of an emphasis on this multipolar disengagement. As soon as he took the reins of power, he resolutely steered Aikido towards a sporting practice with a popular educational and professional vocation. Not to mention a guaranteed economic return which is not the least of motivations for any professional worried about the survival of his "business".

Anyway, putting aside Morihei Ueshiba's descendents ambitions or needs for Aikido for a moment, let's take another look at his influence—and that of the American occupation—on its formation.

MORIHEI UESHIBA: THE DANCING MAGICIAN?

- It must be said here that, if Morihei Ueshiba once excelled in this art of Aiki-jujutsu, with age, the passage of time and experience, he gradually distilled his own technical panorama to create a very special version. The art that he practiced after the war, although remaing very dynamic—and pertinent to perfection at the martial level—had gradually taken on a very personal and refined aspect. It had progressively become philosophically complete for him—truly revealed, if you like—but almost hidden from others: surely the quintessence of the magician's art. And, by philosophically complete, I mean at least in comparison to the Aiki-jujutsu of his old master, Takeda Sokaku. This art remained warlike as well as both culturally and ideologically harsh and severe, and

Takeda must in his old age have seen this step not only with pride, but also with a certain resentment.

It was in 1942 that the decision to call this new art "Aikido" was finally taken and, at that time, although the founder was very nationalist and involved in the war, he was convinced that Japan could not win. And this thinking was reflected in a new conceptualization of his art when he took it in a contemporary direction, full of of movement* and with a "pacifist" vocation—or at least, a proclaimed one.

* *"Aikido is an art of profound significance and, once made available to all, it will spread far and wide, connecting all levels of society, rather than just an elite. Its potential for expansion is boundless." (...) From a letter and a founding text for Aikido since, in it, Kisshomaru presents the "new" activity of Aikido within Kobukai to the authorities after the war. Op. cit., pp. 285. (The full text can be found on pages 270-273 of the Japanese original of Kisshomaru's biography, and on pages 282-286 of the English translation) (...) In the letter, Aikido is presented as an eminently healthy activity to practice, and therefore an activity that is perfectly suited to playing a vital role in Japan's reconstruction. Secondly, concerning the art itself, there is no emphasis at all on atemi striking techniques. Instead, we read that "the movements of Aikido, of defense, are circular, in moving outwards, as in a square, when standing on guard in the form of a cone, in motion as in the centre of a spiral, and while drawing inwards towards oneself. The whole thing is described like a jewel. "The fluid and constantly changing nature of Aikido defies description..." (Op.cit., p. 282.) Thirdly, Aikido is presented as a 'bridging' activity combining the study of health—looking forward to the future—with the traditional art of kagura (explained as ritual dance offered as a prayer) and thus looking back to the past. As such, Aikido builds (Japanese) character and purifies the mind and body. And, importantly, the practitioner can use it to attain the traditional virtues of jujun [柔順: flexibility, also written as 従順], kyogo [強剛: indomitable strength], eichi [叡智: wisdom], and shisei [至誠: sincerity].*

"It should be noted that the meanings of these virtues - Japanese 'virtues' – are 'double-edged' in that they can be paired with vices that they can also become". (Peter Goldsbury-Transmission-Inheritance-Emulation

#28, XV: Aikido et Organisations – Logiciels du Dojo: From Kobukan to Aikikai/IAF).

A number of factors were in play at the time, and they all contributed to the new direction of "development" of this centuries-old "jewel" of an art, all of a sudden idealized right up until 1950 to 1960-1970 and the death of the founder in 1969. Firstly, there was the post-war American policy of "prohibition" of martial arts in general in Japan.* Of course, it wasn't official but, in fact, the Americans wanted to suppress all syndromes of Japanese culture extolling the Japanese warrior spirit (its militarism), and thus avoid any possible new warlike tendencies in the future. Then there was the founder's state of heart and mind as well as his son's and his students' determination to spread Aikido (knowledge) and widen its customer base. Not to mention the very delicate economic, political, social, and cultural situation in post-war Japan.

* Concerning the US occupation: "All traces of militarism and ultranationalism have been ruthlessly swept away, including the Shinto state apparatus; there was a purge of soldiers, policemen, and educational figures; martial arts should were no longer to be taught in schools; and organizations like Dai Nippon Butokukai [大日本武徳会: Great Japan Military Virtue Association] and its affiliates were outlawed. A land redistribution plan was put in place, and the country was firmly on a democratic track with elections—including votes for women—trade unions, and freedom of assembly. Dower and Takemae emphasize that the transformation, while uneven in some respects, was both dramatic and sustainable. (Peter Goldsbury, Aikiweb # Transmission-Inheritance-Emulation #6). Yet Peter Goldsbury also admits that, "The Allied occupation forces made a crucial mistake in 1945, concerning their future plans for Japan: they did not have enough skilled Japanese speakers to take over all the reins of government and had to rely on the defeated Japanese bureaucrats to carry out

their reforms." (Peter Goldsbury, Transmission-Inheritance-Emulation #28, II:吸い物 /Suimono: Establishment of the Kobukai - Some Reflections).

So it is that, with all the respect that is due to Morihei Ueshiba, his magician-like tendency to hide his art from others—*along with Kisshomaru's manifesto letter's "inspired" reference to the traditional dance art of kagura*—engendered the title of this section. But, anyway, tongue-in-cheek inferences aside, let's now leave the subject of the American occupation's influence on Aikido, and turn our attention to its international popularity.

WORLDWIDE DISSEMINATION

 - It was, in fact, only during the nineteen fifties to nineteen sixties that this whole new sporting and technico-philosophically-simplified approach—"The Way of Aiki Educational Pacifism"—began to spread internationally. The expansion was the result of a well organized administrative structure, and of the Tokyo World Centre (Aikikai association) sending young experts to Europe, the Americas, and other countries around the globe. And it was the new populist technical base that allowed it to take place: today, one hundred countries are involved, and there are more than one million practitioners in the world.

Most of these students—especially in the post-war period—had been trained for a few years in this "new" composite style by the founder himself. Then later by his descendants—the "Dochu" or, in Japanese, the "Master of the Way", that is to say Kisshomaru

Ueshiba, as we have seen, and—since 1999—Moriteru Ueshiba (1951-).

The dissemination was also enabled by the Aikikai student teachers, the "uchi-deshi"—salaried live-in students—who were quasi-civil servants of the "big house". They were promised future teaching positions in the framework's outsourced structure: student-teachers... quickly "co-opted as instructors because of the rapidly growing popularity of the art and the vast field of activity of Senyokai-Budo led by Ueshiba (Stanley Pranin, Aikido Journal Editorial, Volume XXIII, No. 4 – 1996". The Senyokai-Budo was the "Society for the Promotion of Martial Arts", founded in 1932 and originally established on the initiative of Reverend Deguchi of the Omoto religion, with Morihei Ueshiba being the chief instructor.

Understanding the confusion caused by the appearance of Aikido instructors that were more "authentic" than others—or looking at the position of direct students of the founder (deceased, 1969)—is not a simple task. However, as a start, it's perhaps worthwhile replacing this human breadbasket with the actual names of those who were direct pupils of the founder (internally, uchi-deshi and externally, soto-deshi) and who are (or have been) mainly known in Aikido as a result of the founder. The list here, although certainly incomplete, is most impressive since all these people are—or have been—recognized as prestigious sensei, in other words, "Masters". They are listed below in alphabetical order with the family name in capitals and, in brackets, the date of beginning of study with the founder or within his educational structures.

ABE Kenshiro (1945), ABE Seiseki (1952), ABE Tadashi (1942), AKAZAWA Zenzaburo (1933), ARIKAWA Sadateru (1947), ASAI Katsuaki (1958), CHIBA Kazuo (1958), COTTIER Ken (1960?), DOBSON Terry (1962), ENDO Seihiro (1964), FRAGER Robert (1964), FUJITA Masatake (1956), FUNAHASHI Kaoru (1931), HASHIMOTO Masahiro (1931), HIKITSUCHI Michio (1951), HIRAI Minoru (1939), TAKUMA* Hisa (1934).

*At first, Hisa Takuma was a pupil of Morihei Ueshiba who, at Takuma's request, taught at the Asahi Newspaper dojo in Osaka. The story goes that one day Takeda Sokaku turned up unannounced at the dojo, saw Takuma, and ended up telling him, "I am Ueshiba Morihei's master. But, you know, I did not teach him everything. To learn everything, you should study with me." And, following this suggestion, Takuma began his apprenticeship with Sokaku to later become the man we all know about. He did not completely abandon Morihei Ueshiba since he participated with him in a sort of classification of Sokaku's Daito-ryu techniques. And it was thanks to him and the articles he published in the Asahi Shimbum newspaper where he worked, that Ueshiba's Aikido began to be really known and sought after.

HOMMA Gaku (1967?), HOSHI Tesshin (1933?), ICHIHASHI Norihiko (1960), IKEDA Hiroshi (1968), IMAIZUMI Shizuo (1959), INOUE Noriaki (1921) (neveu de Ueshiba Morihei), ISOYAMA Hiroshi (1949), IWATA Ikkusai (1930), KAMADA Hisao (1929), KANAI Mitsunari (1958), KATO Hiroshi (1954), KAWAI Reishin (1954), KOBAYASHI Yasuo (1954), KOBAYASHI Hirokazu (1947), KONO Henry (1964), KOYAMA Kenji (?), KUNIGOSHI Takako (1933), KURITA Minoru (1960), KURITA Yutaka (1959), KUROIWA Yoshio (1954), MARUYAMA

Koretoshi (1954), MARUYAMA Shuji (1959), MASUDA Seijuro (1962), MOCHIZUKI Minoru (1930), MURAKAMI Tetsuji, MURASHIGE Morihiko (Aritoshi) (1931), NADEAU Robert (1962), NAKAZONO Mutsuro (?), NISHIO Shoji (1951), NOQUET André (1955), OKA Hiroshi (?), OKUMURA Shigenobu (1938), OSAWA Kisaburo (1939), OYAMA Kunio (?), SAITO Morihiro (1946), SAOTOME Mitsugi (1955), SASAKI Masando (1954), SHIMADA Sakae (?), SHIMIZU Kenji (1963), SHIODA Gozo (1932), SHIRATA Rinjiro (1933), SUGANO Seïchi (1959), SUGINO Yoshio (1932), SUNADOMARI Kanemoto (1942), SUDANOMARI Kanshû (1942), SUGANUMA Morito (1964, TADA Hiroshi (1948), TAKESHITA Isamu (1925), TAMURA Nobuyoshi (1953), TANAKA Bansen (1936), TERADA Kiyoyuki (1948?), TENRYU Saburo (1939), TOHEI Akira (1956), TOHEI Koichi (1939), TOMIKI Kenji (1926), TOMITA Takeji (1962), TSUDA Itsuo (1950), WATANABE Noboyuki (1960), YAMADA Yoshimitsu (1956), YAMANE Sachio (?), YAMAGUCHI Seigo (1947), YONEKAWA Shigemi (1932), YUKAWA Tsutomu (1931).

There are so many others, and my hope is that they will forgive me—especially if they are still alive—for not mentioning them.

In any event, apart from the widely recognized version emanating from the successors and direct instructors affiliated or otherwise with the family line of the founder (Aikikai of Tokyo), many other Aikido branches and trends started by his students, have emerged since Morihei Ueshiba's death. Indeed, many of these students—some of the names in the previous list, moreover—had studied with him at different times in his life, more or less for a long period, and more or less deeply. Or they had also studied other martial arts such as karate, judo, sumo, ko-budo (traditional budo before 1868), sabre and so on.

Each of these students had—after parting ways with him for one reason or another—using his own knowledge, begun to teach the part of the master's wisdom that he'd learned. Or even a new combination linked to his own experience of what he could believe or think of Aiki martiality. So, bearing in mind the plethora of these new schools, the question of what happened next, naturally arises.

THE HYPERONYM AIKIDO - After the

"departure" of so many top teachers and students along with the starting the "Aikido machinery", the story went along the lines of "Telephone the news to your neighbour ...". Then someone who had followed the method of such and such master, taught it "in his own way" to another who himself taught it as he understood it—or couldn't understand it—to a third person. A well-meaning but naive and probably frustrated colleague who, based on what he'd managed to remember, taught it to another who, with his own vision or his personal search for things, has been teaching it to ... and so on.

All this finally gave rise to styles and techniques perceived to be "different" or announced to be so since they had obviously been reconstituted over and over again. And the results—"anamorphoses" or distortions of an original image—were rather akin to Rolling Stones' rock or Chopin played with an Australian native's didgeridoo, a Jew's harp, and competitive tom-toms.

In Japan as in Europe, this is exactly what has happened up until today, with—on top of that—rationalized justifications. In the West, Descartes and Napoleon, and in Japan, the nationalist militarist side of "We don't argue, we obey!" This latter reasoning is the first notion of "Shu-Ha-Ri"*, as we already saw in the presentation on the foundation of "traditional Japanese pedagogy".

* N.B. "Shu-Ha-Ri": "Mime without reasoning" (**Shu**); "Take your independence, learn underlying principles and theory behind the technique" (**Ha**); "Create one's own approach and overcome one's own contradictions by learning from practice" (**Ri**).

While these technical styles or methods can, however, turn out to be expert, it's really not a question of making a judgement on that here. The fact is that, generally, they can all justifiably claim—depending on their original assumptions, feasibility, words, meaning and personalization—to be "famous" or even "authentic". Historically speaking, it has always been more or less this way in Japan, especially in the niche world of martial arts.

The founder of Aikido, Morihei Ueshiba pretty well took the same tack with the inheritance from his own master, Takeda Sokaku, who himself had done likewise. Certainly Takeda had combined his own personal experiences—acquired in his youth and during numerous duels during his initiatory journeys through a still very medieval Japan—with the specific Daito-ryu knowledge that Chikamasa Tanamo, the sonless and last successor of the Saigo clan, had transmitted to him. "Disobedience is the hallmark of man," said one of Seijun Suzuki's heroes in his film *The Elegy of the Fight,* and one could conclude that this is what made the genius in Morihei Ueshiba.

In this way, we might ask ourselves, "Why wouldn't this anarchic extension of Aikido make a legitimate mark for somebody?" Conversely, we might say to ourselves, "Why this "decision" to want to format everything on such an oversimplified frame, and create such a rigid «mold»"?

The answer is quite simply in that these so-called "authenticities"—even if they are real in the sense we've just seen—have had increasing difficulty sticking to the term "Aikido" and its notion of being a "whole" art. Indeed, over the years, Aikido has gradually become fixed in a code as well as in an identity, in its repertoires, its technical forms, its commerce, and in its main lines. This, because—as we have seen—it was deliberately separated from its origins (SokakuTakeda) through the determination of Morihei Ueshiba's successors. However, it wasn't only his successors, but also the determination of the founder himself, and this is an inconvenient wrinkle one doesn't really want to dare even thinking about most of the time. The fact is that, without being mindful of any real motives or grounds—except a desire to make Aikido a hyperonym or umbrella entity in the world of martial arts—a consensus, rightly or wrongly, **absolutely had to be developed**. And this, against all odds, even at the price of great technical or human sacrifices.

In my opinion, Kisshomaru Ueshiba, son of the founder and one of my masters, was the main author of this "decision". And he expressed this in a manner which could not be more clear, when he said, "Aikido should not become a cloisonné art. It must, like kendo and judo, be considered as an art in its own right by all martial arts schools."(Aiki News #81 - July 1989).

As a result of this inflexible quest and the stubborn desire to have Aikido recognized as a "major" art, we can make the observation that, thanks to him and the choices he made, Aikido didn't dissolve into its very many contradictions. In this way, today it even forms an almost stabilized martial arts ensemble that begins to develop its own identity. While many aspects of this outcome can certainly be criticized—even its very own methodology—Aikido is both coherent and certainly not without promise for the future. Therein lies the great work of Kisshomaru Ueshiba and his lieutenants at the time.

In this article, we have tried to clearly state the broad outlines of this Aikido "general law" which when all is said and done, is a consensus on "settling and defining". And this has done while striving not to lose sight of its origins—numerous, novel and relevant but ultimately forgotten—and therefore the contradictions and omissions the astonishing evolution has imposed on us.

But now, let's give some thought to where this Aikido art is going. And in what form.

WHAT KIND OF FUTURE AND FOR WHICH AIKIDO?

- The million-dollar question is will Aikido become a kind of degenerate sports monster like "Ai-judo-ki"? Or will it become a curious mutant, genre "Ai-karate-ki"?

Today, it is difficult to accurately foretell its future, if not to make conjectures. All the same, it is my hope that Aikido can—through the work of its practitioners and masters—take some pleasure in keeping its original Aiki identity. Also, since Aikido really is fantastic, that it can even enjoy rediscovering its origins and, once again, include them in its working panorama as well as in its development perspectives.

This would not be with the idea of becoming—or again becoming—effective, but rather to regain its original, historical and technical legitimacy as well as eliminating its own existential discomfort. And this, not only without departing from the nobility of its appellation and its visionary progress, but also without bad faith revisionism.

As a practitioner of both Daito-ryu and Aikido, I was often asked in Aikido, "What good can Daito-ryu serve?" And, in Daito-ryu, "Is there a difference between Aikido and Daito-ryu?" But to me, Aikido and Daito-ryu have evolved from the very same foundation, namely, Aiki, the original crucible about which I have already talked. *It's just that the philosophical heart that one puts into their practice, is differently enlightened in each one.* Nor is there a hierarchy to establish in the sense of a sharing of knowledge between Daito-ryu and Aikido, or even a sharing of truths. Because at the technical level, there is no breach between these two arts: they have the same trunk! And not only is there a historical continuity, but—equally well—there is an underground lateral continuity. Just like for mushrooms or bamboo, there is a mass of roots or, to use a term dear to the French philosopher G. Deleuze, a "rhyzomic" continuity. And it's this continuity that, in my opinion, we really must bring back to life again.

Up until today, Daito-ryu's isolation has paradoxically managed to preserve the fabulous, historical, and absolutely "Aiki" essence of the art within itself. I mean at the precise and efficient level of Aiki detail, at the real and intelligent technical level of "what connects causes and their effects"—our previous "puppeteering art" I've mentioned—and at the level of the original Aiki spirit.

Aikido itself provides other dimensions to the "extent of feasability of Aiki principles", and these dimensions are those that Daito-ryu has not yet—except at an all-too-rare high level—achieved or wanted to reveal. Among them, we find the following:

- Its **dynamic** aspect;
- Its **popular** vocation;
- Its idea of **wisdom**;
- The novel feature of thinking up the feasible idea of a "**liberating** path*" for other's aggressiveness;
- Its relative **safety** of practice;
- Its vitalist and **invigorating** gymnastics;
- The enjoyable **pleasure** of training, etc.

* *See my first book "Understanding Aikido" (in French), Budo Editions, to grasp and assimilate this fundamental concept of the founder's Aikido.*

I believe it is important to fully appreciate that the multi-conceptual idea of Aikido is, in and of itself, really a great and very profound idea. However, to even further valorize the extraordinary potential of today's Aikido, it's my personal opinion that all Aikido-ka worthy of the name should start to study Daito-ryu one day. That is to say study it or, to the best of their abilities, try to acquire its essence, which, by the way, is not the same thing. The martial arts "tourist" doesn't learn very much in Daito-ryu if he is only motivated by curiosity, if he is graded above fourth dan, or—above all—if he teaches.

However, if they did study Daito-ryu, their Aikido would gain in precision, lucidity, grandeur, calm, efficiency, acrobatic restraint, and especially in legitimacy. And here I'm talking about the legitimacy lost through pedagogical simplifications introduced by past and present administrations, by revisionisms and by artificial reinventions imposed on it. Most notable of these are the "dodges", the "tricks", personal "gimmicks", today's really "bad magician" aspect, and the competitive side of Aikido, genre, "Who is the strongest? "Who is the best?"

But I grant you that it's not so very easy. How can one actually ask practitioners who have been functioning in a certain way for decades, to change their vision of things and put into question "their very own concept of their practice" or their knowledge? How could they question their own self without the risk of losing their aura"—their self-esteem and the esteem they have for others—especially as teachers? That would require one hell of a dose of stubbornness in the search for truth, great strength of character and, above all, considerable modesty. And this is especially true because, in spite of timid attempts at openness, as we shall see in the next section, the essence of Daito-ryu art is still secret to this day.

WHY DOES THE DIVIDE CONTINUE ON?

- The extremely dangerous "jutsu" side of the art makes Daito-ryu too traditional and elitist—and its deepest inner secrets too hazardous—to be revealed to all and sundry. This observation remains valid even though, at present, Daito-ryu has a tendancy to soften the scope of its activity into a less severe and more didactic—in short, more modern—vision of its practice. A vision that often includes more selective sharing of knowledge based on the personal investment capacities of the particular student.

In addition, there is a very considerable margin between the "Daito-ryu movements" taught to beginners or "lambda" students, and "the essence of Daito-ryu" as it can secretly be taught over time to selected students. This corresponds to the traditional and very exclusive principle of Shoden (public), Chuden (master), and Okuden (secret) as well as that of "Mon", "Kishomon", and "Nyumon-sho" documents. These documents involve an often secret "oath of learning", which—at least at a higher level—still exists today in traditional schools. In other words, a disciple's "pact of responsibility" which was once signed in his own blood.

There is still a large margin between the technical teaching of Daito-ryu—its one hundred and eighteen basic techniques, for example—and what it produces in practice and the relationship to the practitioner's body. And while that's really difficult to explain, I believe this is the ultimate point of the "**Ju**" (柔) in "**Jujutsu**" (柔術), in other words, the "sweetness/softness**" of Aiki", a really exceptional concept that I've already talked about. OLIVIER: CHOISIR SVP

The word "**Ekisu**"*—written here in Romaji allowing pronounciation by English speakers—is the Japanese (katakana) word for "extract", and it is used to describe the essence of the art and its "technical crucible". The word essence is employed here in the same manner as it is in, for example, an "essential" oil, not a necessary oil but rather one which alone gathers the qualities, the characteristics, and the power of a substance or plant.

In other words, its inmost nature as opposed to its outward "appearance".

Now the essence of "the art of Aiki"—a concentrate of its constituent character—is not only indisputably formed by its principles, but even more so by the manner in which they can be implemented. A manner which is not "practice in a theoretical unverifiable absolute or vacuum", but very simply one that is "pragmatic in this or that "manipulative" action.

As far as Aiki is concerned, it would be futile to think that only "principles" matter without regard to the very specific way in which they are employed or without the kind of "binary logic" I've already spoken about. It would, in fact, be "the puppeteer's logic"—explained when talking about the eleventh-century Minamoto brothers—but without their possibility of mutual activation which can't be rediscovered either.

* *The Japanese word "**Ekisu**" (エキスou:越幾斯) encapsules "essence", "extract" or "what is exquisite", and is an adaptation of the Dutch word "extract" adopted in the 1600s during the 200-year sakoku seclusion period. The word "extract" comes from the Latin word "extraho" ("to pull out, to extract") which refers to the idea of "bring out" or "withdrawing". But this term has the same or similar origin as, for example, the words "quest", "to quest", "to acquire", "to investigate", and "question", which thus led to the word "exquisite" or "what is sought, delicate, refined" or precisely what is the object of deep and essential research. The etymological combination of these two terms—exquisite and extract—provides the Japanese meaning of the word **Ekisu**.*

So while the divide continues on, the exquisite essence of the art of Aiki possesses the following three parameters, factors that define it along with the conditions of its operation:

- **Kinematic principles of directed use of the human body**—one's own and that of others;

- **The mode** or **specific logic of operation** of these principles;

- **The application and implementation** of these principles.

This is the set of parameters that I call "the essence of Daito-ryu"—the "original crucible" of Aikido—and therefore by direct descent, "the essence of Aikido".

AIKI! - It is my considered opinion that Aikido should only be learned according to this same essence, "the essence Aiki". And this, even if it must then be "adjusted" according to its historical peculiarities, examples of which are the following:

- The contribution of the complex geometric notion of shapes that transform into each other, for example, triangle-to-square-to-circle;

- The contribution of the spiral and the ki-no-nagare as the means and objective of dissipation. In Daito-ryu, however, there's no dissipation, but rather the fastest and, above all, conclusive neutralization. Hence the law of movement in Aiki-jujutsu: "A single tatami, just one second";

- The contribution of an absolutely extraordinary peaceful and vitalistic philosophical plane;

- The contribution of a universality that is simultaneously social, gymnastic, and most enjoyable.

While the reader should understand this list only contains a few examples and is, by no means, an exhaustive one, its brevity does little to diminish the importance of the adjustment I've talked about.

But now let's move on to Aikido's generic laws.

SO WHAT TO DO? AIKIDO'S FOUR GENERIC LAWS
- You may well ask what exactly are the four laws to be implemented—to be put to work—simultaneously and sincerely in our practice to generate a healthy Aikido. By this, we mean, of course, aside from and not to be confused with the minimum absolutely **necessary** qualities, under the conditions previously stated, namely, vigilance, centreing, availability and thoughtfulness. Well, for all techniques we'd like to think of as "Aiki" and those that purport to be "Aiki", the general and historic laws of "**Aiki**" techniques can be stated very easily, as below.

First Law: All or almost all Aiki techniques must work without difficulty when they are implemented by a weaker person upon a stronger person. For example, a child upon an adult, a woman upon a man, an old man upon a young man, or a fifty-kilo person upon an eighty-kilo person, and so on. There is even a basic rule of "one point five", that is to say you must be able to perform the technique without any particular problem or without using particular force on someone up to one and a half times your weight. Success must still be possible up to twice your weight, but it then requires more and more new skills, notably experience, advanced technicality, better use of the Ki or dynamics, and so on. For example, if—with an opponent one and a half times your weight—you find you've problems getting by without special "strengths, speeds or surprises", then you are in the wrong or incorrect Aiki. If not, you are definitely on the right track. It's simple as a personal exam, but we're talking here about much more than just grades. On the other hand, for a bigger person than you, this one-point-five rule does not apply because it's much easier perform Aiki on a person larger than oneself than on a smaller person, i.e. on a person whose chin is above one's head at the moment of attack. And then, of course, the opposite applies. An Aiki which only works on someone weaker proves nothing about Aiki to anyone, except to "believe it", or talk nonsense. In this case, you can better know your limitations by working on your knees, in Hanza-Han-Tachi, and without the excessive kneeling and turning one sees in Aikido.

This first Law is the indisputable basis of judgement of "Aiki", and—by this—I mean of your Aiki and not that of another! But it can also serve as a basis for considering our models of teaching Aikido to children or women. Indeed, I have never, for example, met a child or a woman practicing Aikido under normal conditions (**Shizentai**—see Fourth Law below) who was able to successfully perform a movement as taught, on an adult. On the other hand, I have seen it done and put to the test many times in Aiki-jujutsu.

In Aikido, those who finally manage to get recognition in this very macho world are those who make Aikido masculine with force, speed and surprise! This proves that there is a basic misdirection here, at least in the teaching or in the technical or fundamental theoretical knowledge. Indeed, a movement can be difficult to learn but still easy for anyone to put into effect, at least once its essential execution stages have been assimilated. Otherwise, even if we speak of "Aiki" this or that, it's most often a question of mystification or not an "Aiki" movement at all.

Second Law: An Aiki movement is impossible to thwart or counter during, for example, an attack where a two-handed grab is already firmly in place. This means we can't do "**oozappa**" movements (**oozappa**: 大雑把) as they say in Japanese. (The characteristics of these movements can roughly be described as "as it comes", "in the wave", or "just about anything goes or breaks!") Nor by surprise or force, or at full speed, or all these at once, imagining that, in this approach, lies the foundation of Aiki. This is especially true in the movement's critical phases because then we are finally only camouflaging our problem.

Third Law: In all Aiki forms, injurious joint pain* induced in the partner can never prove anything whatsoever. Rather it's his "astonishment", his impotence, and inability during the whole movement to maintain strong support on his feet. Because, in effect, **right from the start of the first contact**, it's a question of "**De-ai**" or the moment of truth. And at that instant, you must "lead/organize" the body of the partner, opponent, or adversary in a natural way during the development of your own movement, without morphological opposition. This must be done despite the suggestion he may be armed, even if apparently he's not carrying a weapon. And finally done while ensuring you remain in a firm stance throughout your movement, out of reach, but able to strike and even organize angles of imbalance from a secure position.

Fourth Law: All Aiki techniques are "**Shizentai**" techniques in that they are originally planned to be performed by or on the "**Tai**"—the body—in a "**Shizen**" or natural way. As we've already seen, a **Shizentai** configuration—or natural stance—means that the body is prepared to employ such and such efforts or physical exercise. While fitness or the need for a really strong body (**Karada-tsukuri**) should never be overlooked, equally important is the need not to be encumbered by aberrant or false-flag reflexes, literally based on self-defeating attitudes or behaviour. This introduces the very important idea that there are positive and negative aspects to the general behaviour of an individual, in relation to his form of learning.

The positive aspects of Shizentai are:

- Natural body—healthy reflex behaviour, an almost animal faculty of movement;

- Natural body—survival behaviour or going towards the possible and the simple;

- Natural body—multipolar behaviour of bodily intuition. That is to say, going towards a "million colours" of vision of things, and of the tendency to congruence—leading to getting in sync with the surrounds;

- Natural body—dynamic flexibility, general and specific faculty of movement (motricity), targetted according to the effort required. It is of great importance to understand that we're talking here about "needs necessitated by the circumstances".

In other words, natural body leading to active availability of both body and mind or physical and psychic flexibility of exchange (see *My Aikido Memento*).

In contrast, the **negative aspects of a poorly formed body, or one formed by improper training** are as follows:

- Unnatural body—nervous tics, Pavlovian reflexes;

- Unnatural body—aberrant behaviour, going against the possible and the simple, struggling with complexity and confusion, thinking it coherent;

- Unnatural body—binary behaviour or black-and-white reasoning (dualism), genre "I do this, so you do that" (Manichaeism), in other words, movement that is always rational. Rational thinking leading to irrational thinking (genre, convince for good reasons);

- Unnatural body—physical and mental inflexibility or inflexibility of motricity resulting from "customization" or "artificial technical conventions of behaviour".

We can, in fact, summarize or encapsule all of these negative aspects of an unnatural body by describing them as characteristics of psycho-physiologico-rigidity.

Now Aikido (training) today forms practitioners' bodies in a very curious way, and this for ease of use of its repertoire, and therefore according to its own learning or activation "needs". Over the long term, one begins to notice this phenomenon in many practitioners when one visits a few different dojos around the world. Also, in France where Aikido has actually formalized a kind of "bodily convenience" to Aikido that is quite artificial and, moreover, generalised among the more conscientious practitioners, and those who could be described as blinkered.

This false "sharpening" or, if you prefer, toning is both very surprising and most disturbing. It has even become a style, a sort of "trademark" of many masters or teachers of Aikido. However, Master Yamaguchi and many other great masters I've known often insisted on this point of **Shizentai**. And it's only today when I practice in Japan with, for example, visiting French, that I understand why they insisted on its importance. At these times, I am often faced with a practitioner's involuntary sustained spasms in the body and reflexes, which he accepts since he has decided to do so. In this way, French Aikido has—over time—become a very dualist Aikido, angular, brittle and predatory. One comes out of it hurt, struck, bruised and, to put it mildly, with the smile wiped off your face. And this, for what, to show what, to gain what?

It is as if we had reconstructed a martiality described as "specifically Aikido", therefore artificial and almost "concentrationary" aimed at justifying its very value with respect to its own practice. And perhaps compared to other martial arts. For example, the tendency to work karate kicks in recent years—without a single person even knowing what was being done with regard to footwork in Aiki-jujutsu—again shows the competitive approach to the art.

Unfortunately "Aiki" does not work at all in this way. So, if we want to avoid the discomforts of artificial freedom or faculty of movement and body petrification, this really is a point to watch in Aikido teaching. In other words, in **karada-tsukuri**, in practice, a high priority is to safeguard practitioners' **Shizentai**. Although few people realize it, it's important not to form uke who anticipate, for example, Tori movements or those who have "stereotyped" attitudes that correspond to movements they will face. Japanese Sensei pick this up when visiting French dojos and, on their return—for a week or two—their Aikido is more "angry" and more vindictive. Then it resumes its flow, rather like water that has been ill-treated. Often they then discretely make this kind of remark: "What a strange business this is? What on earth are they thinking about when they practice the kind of Akido their sensei teach them … ?"

Anyhow, let's now turn to a discussion of the question of pain that I mentioned before in this section.

NO PAIN, NO GAIN: REALLY? - It
should be recognized that, in Aikido, there are, in fact, two different types of "pain": naturally non-injurious and utilitarian pain; and injurious pain.

Non-injurious and utilitarian pain includes the following:

- Joint aches arising from natural tension, that are not injurious. These aches can become quite painful when they are stimulated but, as soon as the stimulation stops, they dissappear without leaving any after-effects. Nonetheless, Daito-ryu had got a bad reputation because of grimaces uke make during movements in photos or on videos. We don't know for certain just what is the source of these "functional" pains, but fundamentally they are neither hurtful, nor are they the same types of pain as those caused in Aikido;

- The pain related to the exploitation of **Kyusho**, very sensitive points all over the body, most often related to health. To provide an image here, these pains correspond somewhat to those experienced when Shiatsu points—or those used in Seitai therapy to reach a specific body organ—are pressed hard. One can also compare them with a high degree of certainty to that of tensioning in Aikido's yonkyo wrist-control technique, but not specifically to (big fellows') stapling!

- Any aches resulting from atemi. Even made quite forcefully and with impact, if atemi are performed correctly with judgement, they "shock" a stance or allow one to put the partner into a particular bodily configuration without hurting him. This is almost unknown in Aikido.

Injurious Pains. *These are unnatural pains which remain for hours, days, several weeks or months after a lesson, and which can ultimately become chronic. They are **unnecessary** and include the following:*

- Articular pains specifically concentrated and localized only on a mono-articular level—thus on a localized joint—and often not in a folding sense but rather in one of extension. When stimulated, these pains are very hard to bear and remain so even after the stimulation has stopped, often leaving more or less serious after-effects that are locally or non-locally sensitive. Admittedly, breaking a joint may actually be the goal in Daito-ryu or jutsu—these pains are sometimes used in Aiki-jujutsu—but it's almost certainly not the case in Aikido. Older aikidoka all know something about this, but—curiously—they have never asked themselves any questions about it. Besides, today's Aikido unfortunately works mainly on this type of pain, and you only have to watch how a movement—**Juji-garami**, for example—is made, to understand this. It's terrible, it's horrible, and it's stupid "to cause uke to move or to fall because he's being hurt." But without in any way putting his body under natural strain: the difference between "twisting" and "winding", between "pinching" and "grasping", and between "lever" and "wrenching", and so on. This means that, if he is armed, it will probably breaks his wrist or something like that, but in reality, the danger hasn't been removed. On the contrary, in fact, it will be increased by his anger and the potential of his use of further weapons;

- Injurious pains can also arise from atemi made forcefully impacting certain vital body points or made recklessly, improperly, violently, or awkwardly. Equally well if they are made with a "non-Aiki", destructive aim of simply destroying… something that has no place in Aikido.

To summarize then, pain(s) that an Aikido movement can cause must not be an objective in and of themselves—they're a route—and must not be a justification, nor a proof, and—even less so—cause an injury. This is because the pain induced by an Aikido movement is "**functional**" in the sense that it is a means of **mobilizing** the partner. It can indeed serve to provoke his collapse—kote-gaeshi, for example—or, due to his nervous reaction, help stop him during a powerful attack like ryo-kata-dori. And finally it can force him into a particular bodily attitude, allowing one to more easily perform one's own movement, for example, entry on an attack in Gyaku-hanmi katate-dori or Yokomen-uchi.

So much for the pains, and their place in the martial art that we practice. But now it's time to summon up all of these themes that we went through during this exciting historical journey, and to conclude on some kind of more comprehensive interpretation.

CONCLUSION

So, as we have seen, there are the four general laws that should be born in mind by all practitioners who seek the truth that lies within the "Aiki Crucible".

In my opinion, the issue of knowledge here arises to a lesser degree for the "novice" practitioner than for teachers, and for those already climbing the "dan ladder" which skews all data on the problem of Aikido's legitimacy. A philosopher, a surfer, or a musician would smile and say that nothing changes under the sun, and that our civilization rightly injects myths into our lives. Myths to which we are asked to conform to the detriment of our autonomy, our ontology, our right to know, and often our freedom to aspire to "authenticity".

Yes, that's it. That's the heart of it. I think we must keep a cool head, and therefore a critical attitude towards scenarios and customs often served up to us like artificial pap on a silver platter. Certainly, faced with all that is to be discovered about fundamental Aiki, these scenarios and customs are hardly the most important since they are only frameworks of approaches, not its essence. In other words, the container and not the content with the proviso, of course, that, as for a good bottle of wine, there wouldn't be a good content without a suitable container and a "label" easily permitting its identification!

So, as the hunters say, let's make every effort to avoid confusing the shadow and the prey. In other words, let's distinguish between gruel and gastronomy or, if you prefer, between the theory of likelihood and the theory of the truth. And this, in as far as is possible, without giving full sway to our reasoning which is admittedly most often lacking in matters concerning "the ancient and real way of Aiki thinking".

This is not because there is no reason to put it (our reasoning) into play, but because, contrary to what one would have us believe, there are reasons that this or that judgement isn't yet able to comprehend—nor, above all, see—or unfortunately understand, and therefore not yet know or recognize.

BE BRAVE! - Anyway, rather than reason, I would prefer to say, "Sapere Aude" (Latin proverb) or "Have the courage to make use of your own understanding". On this issue, I believe it would be good for every practitioner—with simplicity and honesty—to make allowances for things as well as for the inconceivable, which often becomes reality. And that he do this, not only with the means he finds available on his way, but above all with those he himself seeks with all his heart, tooth and claw. And I would say that—whatever his style—one day soo, he use his own understanding to make himself—through his Aikido—autonomous, authentic, and humble before history. And lastly, smiling with a healthy body, honest, and unswerving, in other words, true and authentic in its sweetness (jujutsu 柔術).

THE PHILOSOPHY OF AIKIDO

INTRODUCTION - The founder of Aikido, Morihei Ueshiba, was a man deeply involved with the Japanese religious practice of Shinto*. As a brilliant innovator, he was a kind of shaman with such a complex discourse that his contemporaries often had difficulty understanding him. And this, to such an extent that, most of the time, he was incomprehensible even for his closest students. In fact, he really was a visionary and, in many fields, a forerunner.

"Shinto" religion: literally, "The Way of the Gods". The word "gods" in this context is to be taken in the sense of the all-present "kami" (spirits in English) or "the essence of all things". Also note that Shinto is the traditional Japanese animist religion, in other words, one that maintains that objects, places, and all living things possess a distinct spiritual essence.

Ueshiba Morihei had a very specific way of viewing the world and of contemplating Aikido along with the way he believed it was imparting a new form of humanity to the world. Didn't he once declare that "Aikido was not born of religion", but that Aikido could "illuminate religion and guide past teachings (...) towards their completeness"? It is not, therefore, a religious discourse that one must think about while contemplating his work. Rather, there is something else in his journey—a project greater than one would think—because, for the founder, Aikido allowed the individual to finally return to his "true self". In other words, to the divine and unique that lies within each one of us or, in Japanese, *motogaeri*, meaning the return to one's spiritual origin. In this respect, Aikido was also very far from some kind of simplistic pedagogic or educational system. In fact, it was so far removed from any ordinary moral dimension and other kind of social concern that it stood out and went far beyond any mystico-religious aim or discourse.

In fact, Morihei Ueshiba recalled that even "The most religious of today's guides don't provide any way of accomplishing or realizing their ideals". *And this is as technically valid as those sensei who say, "Work with your hips", but who do not say how to do it in practice.* And it is precisely that which, according to him, takes away from them any "way of gauging their own understanding". However, it is the very gauging of this "understanding" that is so very important for the simple reason that an ideal which remains just an ideal doesn't know where its own thinking can lead the world. The word "understanding" is therefore an active word—a word that chases the ideal out of dreams, religion out of revelation—and not an abstract one that would only signify "to end up knowing". Rather it implies the idea of taking possession—grasping, in a sense—of this world and, at the same time, because of one's illuminated state, an ataraxic* use of this world.

* *Adjectival form of ataraxia or peace of mind, serenity, the absence of trouble.*

In this way, Morihei Ueshiba placed Aikido on a novel level of validity, a method of fulfillment and of self-realization beyond this world. But, as we shall soon see, his successors had another "way" in mind.

OBJECTIVE VALIDITY OR DELIRIOUS POMPOSITY - We have seen how Ueshiba Morihei placed Aikido on a novel, more spiritual level of validity. Nevertheless, over time, his many and varied successors transfered Aikido to much more mundane levels, such as the popular, sporting, or the commercial, for example. In such cases, this development marked the loss of a very large part of the authentic sense of serenity (ataraxia) one could derive from Aiki—and thus from Aikido as practical application of a stream of philosophical thought. It is my belief that, despite seductive discourse similar to O Sensei's bygone messages—messages I'll better define later—the messages themselves have effectively become foreign to many who today claim, officially and with great pomp, to be representatives of "The Aikido of Morihei Ueshiba".

However, for the founder of Aikido, the way or path of the warrior (**Bu-do**) was and remained forever a sacred path or way expressed as "**shobu-aiki**"* or the budo that creates wisdom, judgement and the mind of a sage. And it is this word—this concept of "sacred"—which can untether Aikido from the purely spiritual, orienting it in a distinctly philosophical direction.

*"*Shobu-aiki*" 聖武 合 気 *or "the sacred warrior of the Aiki"; also Tenjin-goitsu* 天人合一*or "Man and heaven are one" (Tao); and Kannagara* 神 神*or "to become like the spirit of a god" (Shinto).*

This articulation of the sacred towards wisdom offers a route towards a form of **reverance** for the **absolute**

value of evolution in ourselves. And here, "absolute value" means the unchanging and sufficiency of all human being's particularly human character or what we could call "the essence of us". Using this approach, it is today possible to separate Aikido philosophy from the thorny, pseudo-argumentative and highly stammering bug of the much-loved "post-Morihei-Ueshiba Aikido".

And it is, I believe, at this point that my apparently exaggerated concern in wanting to better define "a philosophy of Aikido" already reveals itself as being much more serious and, above all, less ingenuous than it seemed.

"ESSENCE" YOU SAID? - The essence which we've talked a bit about, may be conceptualized quite well using common sense, without reference to reason or judgement. In fact, it isn't only expressed as a form of abstract thinking, ethereal reflection, or purely intellectual exercise. It's not a trivial game we're talking about here, and it's not gossip either, nor is it a subject of a bar conversation with a friend. This essence is expressed—or should be expressed—by its application in the dynamic practice of this "will for permanent constructive conciliation or concordance at the centre of confrontational movements". Or as William Gleason put it in his book *The Spiritual Foundations of Aikido* (page 49), "dynamic exchange between opposite polarities which arise continuously from the unity of the infinite".

Indeed, it's the practical application of this concordance to seemingly paradoxical circumstances which marks its sufficiency, and therefore its true validity, both martial and philosophical. For it's the detoxification aspect of this application that engenders—brings on, if you prefer—the revelation of this essence of us, this unchanging centre of action and of our own being, on which cause-effect relations depend. It releases it—or rather should release it—from its overlay of misrecognition and indifference. In this respect, the vulgarly classic discourse on, for example, harmony*—quite abstract and very hollow, but very common in Aikido—can easily become a pretext, a decoy, a "catch-all" or even a sort of skylark-catching mirroir. And one that actually stimulates nothing at all of the essential Aiki as such, or of that ontological and ataractic essence that Aikido can bring us to discover.

*Harmony cannot, couldn't exist only by a "putting in sync" of the human being with a creative intention going beyond the material order itself. According to Kotodama—the divine spirit within words—that's the reason why it's better to speak of **harmonics**. Harmonics in the sense of "vibration whose frequency is an integer multiple of another frequency, rather than of "harmonies", sounds pleasing to the ear". Without wishing to play on words here, there is in that a route to be made from "reasoning" to "resonance".*

So we see, Aikido is not therefore "the result of a spiritual discourse", but rather "the result of setting in order—arranging if you like—of a pragmatic and real understanding of a direction which is itself spiritual". In addition, this understanding we're talking about must be experienced as "experiential understanding" or "experiential sensation". That's why, when we practice with partners, in effect, we practice this experimentation on ourselves.

Now, when we say experimentation, we do mean experience, and thus the exercise of research and harmony—both voluntary and permanent—on the subject of this experience. In fact, one could even say, "from the subject to the experience". More generally, this subject of experience is Aiki or the eternal reciprocal creative concordance (not harmony) of Yin (water) to Yang (fire), expressed by the Japanese symbol In-Yo or, in Chinese, that of Yin-Yang. In all confontational circumstances, Aikido naturally establishes itself from this fundamental study base: starting right from the induction point and confrontation within one's interweaving with another, and vice versa. And this, in a **simultaneous, necessary** and **contingent** manner.

The risk then in talking about a "philosophy of Aikido" is that any discussion of Aikido or its practice—instead of being didactic and Socratic or maieutic—can easily morph into a confused ensemble of grand gestures and theoretical or demagogic results without any relation to what should be lived in practical reality.

This observation is particularly valid if these delusiary effects continue to be the results of speculative understanding, of meaningless words, misused words or words whose significance is confused or ignored. And here, among other things, I think of the many and difficult problems of translating Japanese into French or English, or even the confusion arising from words spoken vaguely in one's own langage. These linguistic activities can often lead to futile or false opinions and thus—in the present context—reducing thinking about Aikido to arbitrary judgments or to statements of pure "intentions of principles".

CONCEPTION / SUBSTANCE -

Fortunately, we have just seen that the philosophy of Aikido stems from a form of expression other than that of words. It is, in fact, a form of conceptual expression given material form by experiential body practice. In theory then, this can end up by unambiguously providing the proof of its truth, of its authenticity—or otherwise—and therefore of its true possibilities.

As for the materialization of this philosophy—as much as that of this practice—it is the "Do" (道)or path of learning that will provide a "framework". Aiki training is, in fact, carried out in a topology that we visualize as "a way", a "path", or an initiatory track that—over the years—one must try out or experience and therefore, because of its very nature, travel along. So we are talking about a "philosophy in action" here—not a "philosophy of action"—and it is most important to understand this vital nuance. In this way, we can say the philosophy we can deduce from Aikido here is one of the few "applied philosophies" of the modern world.

But here too, we must ask ourselves what do we mean by "a way"? Well, it is first and foremost a method of secure practice established within a luxuriant context, namely that of martiality as far as Aikido is concerned. This "way", path or Do is then followed—carried out, if you like—in a dojo (training room) on tatami mats (formerly made of straw) within a framework of exercises and hypotheses of standardized work. This "way" is here the experiential framework—physical, physiological, decisional and structural—of Aikido's research process. In other words, according to the definition of Daruma, the Buddhist monk Bodhidharma: "martial arts practice is a prayer of the body".

But, on the other hand, the discovery of its principles will mainly come from from the respect we observe towards the absolute value of our own evolution within this framework. Indeed, as William Gleason points out, "practice is the tool ... of the study of principles*".

Page 113 of his work "The Spiritual Foundations of Aikido", G.Trédaniel Editor, French version.

ONLY A TOOL, ONLY SOME PRINCIPLES

In terms of principles, this Aikido philosophy has stayed as it was at its inception—a **Tao**, the Chinese word for way, path or road—and it stands out, remaining far from our usual Western reference points or formating. For example, it is alien to our Judeo-Christian conditioning which thinks of the world in Manicheistic terms—a duality of good and bad. It is therefore—in stark contrast to a religion—in no way the activation of a good (a kindness) that should be done and an evil that should be fought (justice). Or even worse, of an evil that should be forgiven.

There is no parallel to be drawn between In and Yo—in Chinese, Ying and Yang—and Good and Evil. That would be absurd since In and Yo is **trinitarian** and **not binary** (In-Mu-Yo: 3-9-6), and moreover, In and Yo have relational values. They are precisely two polarities articulated around a "keystone", elements of the same ensemble in a dynamic and perpetual movement towards creation of a completeness. This principle being that of change and thus the energising principle or function of oneness. And this, in sharp contrast to the idea of Good and Evil which artificially constructs opposing values*, separating the world into two distinct and conflicting parts.

The last message of the founder to his students was very clear on this point: "Man has selfishly created the sense of good and evil, and has forgotten the very essence of his true nature" (extract). One cannot better define a **Tao,** nor explain the extent to which a **Tao** differs from a division of the world between good and evil!

** The **In or Yin** is determined by its complementarity to the **Yo or Yang**, and vice versa. The two are thus formed by their synergy. Good, on the other hand, is determined by its eternal confrontation with evil. Each one of these two—good and evil—can, in fact, only be constructed on struggle and destruction or alternatively, by forgiveness of its opposite.*

If one wants to think about, practice and clearly define Aikido, it is—philosophically speaking—a blind alley to want to enter the wilderness of mirrors that is "good and evil".

There is neither good, nor evil, nor fairness to be found in Aikido since, if "honour" has a meaning in Japan, the principle of "fairness" in combat is completely and utterly foreign to Japanese martial arts and, in general, those of Asia. Fairness of means—fair play, for example—really has no sense as a concept in Japan. The principle of balance of forces to fight "fairly" just doesn't hold water: in warlike Japan, winning is all that matters, and the means are of little consequence.

The general principle of Aikido is similar to this but much more complex than one would think in that there is no longer any ethical, technical or suitability limitations to respect on the number of means one can employ. So, having learned the nature of Aikido's freedom—lack of constraints, if you prefer—we will now go on to see how the art expresses itself at the pre-philosophical level.

THE ROLE OF SHOBU-AIKI - As I have already mentioned, the founder of Aikido himself spoke of "shobu-aiki", that is to say, the "Bu-do or martial way that creates wisdom and judgement or the mind of a sage". This is another excerpt from the lecture given by Morihei Ueshiba for the Byakko-Kai organization, and recopied in his book *Takemusu Aiki*. And it is this other very important point—the old sacred become profane—which directs Aikido towards philosophy.

In fact, it is by this kind of reflection that Aikido actually begins to express itself on a pre-philosophical level. It is therefore the "true nature of man realized through his Aiki"—his potential for permanent **conciliation** or adjustment to the world, both specifically and generally, in an aimiable, conscious and enlightened manner—which must quickly become the research tutor in Aikido.

And it is this search for the purpose of being—the self if you prefer—that is fundamentally the general and active principle of Aikido's philosphical undertaking. When we speak of "self", we mean something quite different from self-pride—the "I" which speaks constantly but says nothing but of himself. No, we mean the "original, essential self"—almost independent of our material being—in search of itself in the world.

In this way, each training session serves to direct the practitioner—or should direct him—a little more towards this sincerity ("makoto" 誠 in Japanese) and a creative self-calming ("sunao" 素直 in Japanese) or "peaceful unity". And towards a vital detachment from the heart of this world ("mushin" or "mu-no-shin", 無心 in Japanese), in other words, a state of no-mindness where the mind, not fixed on any thought or emotion, is totally available or alert.

However, the word "conciliation" that we have used previously never means "weakness" or "compromise" but rather signifies "to make legitimate" and "to make precise". That is to say, finally, "to make **relevant**", and this is something one really has to understand as well.

It implies a level of knowledge, a sort of territory of awareness that is potentially known, controlled. In effect, it is just as possible to be germane in a majority

"In" (Ying) as it is in a majority "Yo" (Yang) or similarly, at a mid-point of imbalance or tipping point between the two, for example. *It all depends on the circumstances and not on "judgment" at all*, and **this explains why**—but few practitioners understand this point—**there is basically no dualistic moral principle in Aikido**.

But this mastery comes—and can only come—from the body: Aiki and its principle cannot really be discovered without effort and permanent exercises as well as an exactness and precision. For sure, Aiki is a natural initiative, but it is one that demands a search for knowledge (the right one) and the associated body training, so it can be put in place consciously and always appropriately. This plurality of relevance does not, however, place itself "above" others: again, it doesn't judge but rather acts within its own measure or capacities. And, as we have seen, this "measure" is intrinsically—by definition, if you like—always sufficient, inherent to its own potential of unity.

On this issue, I like to repeat that Master Endo—during an internship in France a few years ago—strongly reminded us that, in Aikido, it was good:

− Not to lose direction--**Mayoanai**--迷わない

− Not to doubt--**Utawanai**--疑わない

− Not to be surprised--**Odorokanai**--駭かない

− Not to compete--**Arasoanai**--争わない

This philosophical formulation was not even translated into French, nor really taken up elsewhere later. Was its depth even understood or grasped? Somehow, I don't really think so.

All the same, the philosophy of "The Way of Aiki" does take its place in the "sphere" of this kind of will or determination. It's already inherent in the intention to be "different", to see oneself and to live one's life "differently". This philosophy takes its place on the plane of determinism—the natural law of In and Yo— to become a living embodiment of Aiki at the heart of any critical research mapping or of any personal journey. And this is where, in Aikido, we ebb and flow between **ontological** levels—questions about the nature of what we are—and **ethics**, in other words, questions about the way of being, the way we should live.

AIKIDO: A DIFFERENT WAY OF THINKING

- In the very idea of Aikido, there is therefore an extremely powerful "thinking differently" or, as we would say today, "thinking outside the box". For example, Takeda Sokaku went to Okinawa to "test" the martial skills of the Chinese art of the hand, karate, a newcomer to Japan at the beginning of the twentieth century. When he met its representatives, he didn't think, "What can Aiki do against these types of fighters? On the contrary, he thought: "What could these people do against Aiki?". This is one way, for example, to "think differently".

Now, let's return to Master Endo's important landmark words—"**Do not lose direction, do not doubt, do not surprise, and then do not compete**". By giving them a positive spin this time, they become more open and understandable to us Westerners, and the boundaries they determine become beneficially "porous" and receptive to exchange. In this way, as can be seen below, they evolve into a very interesting "volume" of work.

Do not lose direction	⇔ **FIND ONE'S GOOD DIRECTION**
Do not doubt	⇔ **HAVE CONFIDENCE**
Do not be surprised	⇔ **BE PREVENTIVE**
Do not compete	⇔ **COOPERATE**

Without being in the least bit embarrassed then, by placing ourselves in the midst of a completely secular and inter-relational environment, we return in an imposing way to what we talked about at the beginning of this section. That is to say, by its practice *and above all, by an understanding of this practice*—and because the practitioner gradually rediscovers the source of everything in himself—Aikido enlightens human learning and knowledge towards their fullness.

Aikido must thus allow the individual in a very real way—practice-to-reality-to-calming—and in an increasingly stable way to touch on—reach, if you think better— "the true self". And this to the point of transcending it.

Now, "the true self" is a totally balanced, stable form of power, not a form or type of force. These two things are different, although the difference is only rarely understood. Yet this difference again offers a very good explanation of why the gauging of the action in Aikido can always be sufficient*.

* While force in Aikido can be likened to an ascending curve, power in Aikido is never limited in the sense of its expansion. That is to say, since it is not limited in its infinite possibility of whirling round between its positive and negative form—a bit like the ever-moving sweeping trace of a radar screen—its equation would not be that of a curve but rather a circle or an ellipse. Likewise, in Japanese, the word "force" is designated by the word "chikara" 力 (or ryoku) whose depiction is the force of a fist or of a nerve-controlled force. Equally well, in Japanese, force can be designated by the word "tsuyoï" 強, whose depiction—this time, completely different—is one that represents the association of a bow with an insect, signifying rather "the intensity of a force". Power, on the other hand, is depicted by words that always include the symbol of force (chikara/ryoku 力) but, since these words are usually associated with another concept, power always goes beyond force. For, since power is, by definition, composite—combining different architectures or materials—it becomes indeterminable, at least in absolute value. And we see this in the words "ken-ryoku" 権力 (the authority of a power, its influence and its right), "tai-ryo ku" 体力 (physical potential force, vigour)," sen-ryoku" 戦力 (the military force) and "kyo-ryoku" 協力, the cooperation of a cluster of thirty forces, or, more interesting here, "kyo-ryoku" 強力, the power = the combinaison of different forms of forces), etc.

To put it more succinctly, we're talking here about "power" and not simply about a "force", a "force" in general, or even about "some forces of ...this or that".

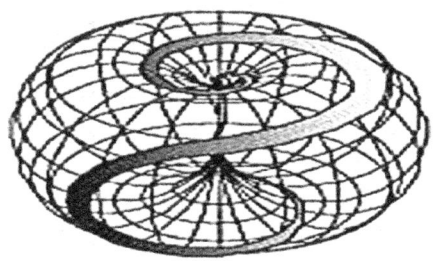

DIVINE IN THE MAYONNAISE? -

Now let's really get the ingredients to work here. The founder of Aikido talked of "touching the divine that is within each one of us"—a "divine" which we understand as also being a power and not a force. Equally well, we understand the word "touch" since it corresponds to ancient Aiki-jujutsu techniques and to those traditional techniques concerning the body in general, traditional medicine, for example.

This also characteristic of the animal side of human beings that transcended or evolved—went beyond, if you prefer—from "man" into "Man" (*ningen* 人間 in Japanese*) which to the Japanese precisely signifies "society or man as a purely social being". And in effect this power is not limited since, to varying degrees, it is made up of all other forms of power, those possible and those one can only imagine.

* *In Japan there is an informal hierarchy of human types—men and women included—which continues through time and its history. This hierarchy is, moreover, still commonplace in Japanese society and its* *values, even if it never expresses itself openly. So people are more or less classified into these categories, with ascending value:*

- *A **"thing"**: mon 物 (a male or female "anything", a thing, a kind of all, yet nothing at the same time);*
- *A **"nothing"**: kuzu, Kuzuya 屑屋 (insulting term. This is "a gatherer of dust", somebody that doesn't really exist, a name that says nothing to anyone);*
- **Someone**: *dareka だれか Daremo だれも or Daredemo だれでも (anyone, someone who can be replaced by anyone);*
- *An **individual**: mono 者 (someone with a name who, if not integrated into society, can still have a function, or live independently);*
- *A **person**: hito 人 (a person who has a business card, a position, a function or a social position);*
- *A **human being**: ningen 人間 (someone who has rights and who assumes his duties);*
- *A **"sacred or a divine man"**: shinin, shinjin or kamito 神人 (someone who has perfectly linked his soul to his state of being human and who, as such, is human close to the gods.*

And we understand here the fundamental purpose of "Do"—the Way—and that is to lead practitioners, in as far as is possible, to climb this Japanese scale of values!

Through this purely philosophical approach, "divine" here becomes the word that best describes Man's essential reality. Not a religious or metaphysical determination of mankind in general, but rather the reality of his essence—an essence to be rediscovered and directed in a newly original sense.

Since this goes beyond all contingencies—in other words, uncertain future circumstances—external to Man himself, he—as a living being—reaches maximum availability, maximum centering, maximum alertness and maximum attentiveness. Clearly, he becomes absolutely "centred" or central and yet absolutely "available" or open. In other words, we see Man open to all, participating in his environment yet liberated from its coercive, restraining and unforseen aspects. And not only that, but taking some satisfaction in the liberty.

Just the same, let's be cautious when making these comments since we mustn't make a mistake of interpretation. Here "liberated" doesn't mean Man can do "what he wants" but rather "what he should do" and, among other things, what he must do to keep that liberty. This is because, since these contingencies naturally continue to impact or frustrate him constantly, it is necessary to "work", to train and to study directly and consistently the purpose of confrontation and martiality. The aim here is to be able—as much as is possible—to "unhook" or to somehow go beyond—we'll see how later—this state of dependence on events. So yes, of course, unhook "oneself", but it's also necessary for these liberated "ourselves"—through our own influence and its diffusion in the world—to unhook our world from its own baseness as well.

As we shall soon see—and as I mentioned in my first book on Aikido *Understanding Aikido* (French text, Budo-Éditions)—there are other very interesting routes towards this type of "Aiki martiality" to discover.

THE "TRUE SELF OR NON-SELF" -

The discovery of the "true self" is an instant attainment, an awakening or enlightenment, that is not achieved by grasping—the self in action—but rather by letting go. And it could be thought of as one imbued with balance and **adequacy** or, if you prefer, reasonableness.

It must be said here that, if this ethical attainment with its ontological association is also involved with society, none of society's "glittering prizes" can surpass it in any way whatsoever. And this, because it involves something much more than an investment, more important than the ostentatious world of titles and vanity. It is the investment and rediscovery of the being that we are—for oneself, in front of oneself and in front of the world. And this, for each of us in a personal and unique way—even if the specialness of each one of us is connected to all the "worlds" which surround us. Aikido is precisely directed at the experimentation and the practical outcome of the individual's attainment of a state consistent with "each within the whole" and "the whole within everyone".

In this sense, the philosophy of Aikido is an active and essentially bodily philosophy. That is to say, it emanates not from a reflection or a distortion of the reason at the base, but rather: from the work of the body to the training (more and more deep, to the point, if possible to come to embrace reason). In this way, "from the body" will spring the experimentation and essences of the true of life.

I will not, therefore, enter into a so-called "relevant" critique of our world, of our civilizations, of our ways of life. I do not want to start a political discussion, or a counter display of "knowledge" that I absorbed or willpower since my birth.

To yourself, if you wish, to invent your own political, geopolitical, economic, social, environmental analyzes ...

Indeed, the look "that looks good", or, says : "wisdom", can come, in my opinion, from "the life of the body, finally: who lives and expresses part of this life which he finally assumes, the wisdom of the natural laws of the world (laws which concern: time, space, cycles, emptiness, balances, etc.) ".

Thus : "to do", "to do it", "to be able to do it": "the gesture", is always a prerequisite and a condition for validating the words we are going to say, that we will write (the famous: "to be able to say what we do and do what we say!"). And especially for Aikido.

The rest is only opinions, so uninteresting. Finally ... No, I mean: interesting sometimes informative often, certainly. But ultimately of little value in terms of veracity. If not, and this is their interest, as an indirect revelator of "who is who and how? ". Or revealing as links and social connections (which is fundamentally important also on a human scale, I grant you).

Then, how we define more simply this, and although understanding it seems a little long, each step is fairly simple, and the first concept to grasp is that all life is one. And by this, I mean that all things and living things from viruses and bacteria, microbes, red ants and blue whales, peonies and baobabs, grasshoppers and hippopotamuses, and animals in general and humans - are composed of the same kinds of trillards and trillards of trillards of tiny energetic atoms and the same "life force". Of course, their atomic arrangements differ. Thus, in animate beings, eating and reproduction differ, duration of life varies, and the degree of consciousness varies, but it's always the same atoms and the same life force. And whatever the length of life, all living things just seem to want to persevere on living (B. Spinoza).

Scientists are now close to understanding the mechanism by which over three million years ago, an inanimate atomic compound—a set of molecules agglomerated in a particular assemblage, and in particular environmental and energetic conditions—had a life opportunity, like "hatch at the first beat of life", and so began to live. In other words, to nourish oneself, to breathe, to grow, to move autonomously, and of course to: reproduce.
However, this orderly life of "continual challenges" lasts only a moment on the astrological scale for every living being. But this "life" is repetitive, and multiplies on massive scales of time and space (often unimaginable for us: some living beings today, bacterias or algaes for example, live on Earth almost since the beginning of its creation). However, while scientists know that this life force exists, they are far from knowing "why" it is activated. And researchers are even further from understanding exactly what "life" is. But, mirage, holographic matrix, or material reality, one way or another (?), it exists. Also because we experience it every day

While all human beings and living things die—many as a cycle of exchanges and regeneration to give food to other living things more often than not—the billions of billions of energetic atoms that make them up are, to varying degrees, recycled, many of them turning up in other living things which, of course, also have the life force within them. In fact, these atoms are so astronomically numerous and—eventually, in some cases—so widely spread around in the world that you unknowingly may have a few of Alexander the Great's atoms in you. But not some from John Lennon because not enough time has elapsed!

Morihei Ueshiba said, like many oriental traditions, that: "Each of us is a miniature universe*, is a living shrine". Thus, although we seldom know it, each of us lives "life" in his body as a small universe in himself: innumerable atoms in fact rush and constantly exchange within each of cells that make up our "being alive" (12 billion cells in a human body, and one hundred thousand billion bacteria that swarm in our intestines for example). But above all, we live "life" as a permanent exchange. We receive as much as we disperse, constantly receiving, information, energies, and materials to all other living and non-living things around us, in our environment, and within the universe.

---

* *Inside each of these metropolis-like cells, along with fixed DNA, there are countless billions of atomic compounds—including enzymes and proteins—zooming around and effortlessly doing the vital creative and maintenance work necessary for life. They are powered by energy from a billion ATP "battery packs"—chemical energy from the atoms' electrons—continuously created by mitochondria (ancient bacteria combos) from oxygen and the food we eat. And these ATP—integral* *elements of the life force—also provide the energy for our bodily movement (→ki).*

All this activity takes place as we not only constantly exchange messages with all other living and non-living things making up our environment, but also dynamically exchange non-living matter with other living things in our environment, namely breathing and eating. For example, although we don't "see" it, without the oxygen in the air from the rain forests and sea plankton—it's their "waste"—we could not live for more than a few minutes, and the trees feed off the used air we breathe out, our own waste.

Now, although these atoms of which we are made have energy, they do not live properly, and are probably unaware of anything (such as the components of a clock, they just seem to obey random or mechanically organized laws of the universe - the search for its laws being in the field of physics, astrophysics, theosophy, or spiritual research -). But we, humans - by this vital force that is in us and thanks to our evolution - have become aware to a certain extent non-negligible (we still have great progress to make I think!). We are aware of ourselves and our environment, conscious of other living things and inanimate objects around us (for example we are aware of the existence of atoms, molecules, bacteria or viruses, and to inverse: cycles of the planets, the existence of distant galaxies ...).

While that environment is not exactly "harmonious*" (in the sense of an arrangement between the parts of a whole that contribute to the same purpose), sense, it is—as we have seen—a self-regulating complex system composed of an infinitesimally large number of interdependent "living and non-living parts" locked in a constant, ever-changing, dynamic and sometimes violent equilibrium. A system that, until now, has maintained optimal conditions for every "living" thing to continue on living with the proviso.

* Why did I say, "without being exactly harmonious"? Because the disappearances of the primary era, for example large forests (about 500 million years ago), or the disappearance of the dinosaurs at the end of the Cretaceous (66 million years ago) should bring us to a little more relativism on this subject of harmony in nature, since we know neither its purpose!

To return to Ueshiba Morihei and likewise in a similar way, the Japanese Shinto religion maintains that "kami"—spirits or the essence—are in all living and non-living things in the world and share all its interrelated complexity. Now, while many scientists point out how much incredible it is that our immediate environment, the Earth, is so perfect for human beings and other living things to live in, is to look at the King-Man to the Servile Earth with some naivety.

We have indeed evolved from molecules composed of atoms which contracted and created the vital force, and we are made of and have in us organism that are over a million years old. We developed along with the Earth's living and non-living environment, and it's normal the Earth seems perfect for us. So, however we choose to think about it, we are both "in" and "of our" environment: and it is this environment that has conditioned our evolution.

And this is what is meant by "each within the whole" and "the whole within everyone". It is a seamless, transparent, repetitive integration (in two-way), of the tiniest to the most humongous.

Thus, this dual property becomes "fundamental non-change despite the scales discussed". This can be likened to fractal properties (as in mathematics, where a change of scale in a fractal equation does not vary the plot of its curve, even complex). But do not worry about it, it's this idea of "double integration" both to the infinitely small (Shin) and at the same time to the infinitely big (Ten) that counts.

"Dis-integration"? From our environment, Humanity blinded by its "civilizing" discovery of the Age of Enlightenment* has gradually lost its respect, its wonder, and its fear for the Earth and its inhabitants, animated or otherwise—its simple and complex components—. In fact, humanity has lost its real place which was, as the Amerindians claimed before their near-massacre, " The guardian and protector of the worlds of creation on Earth ". Respect for other human beings has been lost, or respect for their local, traditional or ancestral values.

Age of Enlightenment: typically Western philosophical current that declares the new man Demiurge (Man became God), and science become his new religion in the heart of his power (a totally atheistic religion: what a paradox!).

Thus, the human being, while believing himself more "intelligent" than the other living beings of the creation, has not at all become wiser: it is the only living being for example which produces, at the end of one generation (about 80 years old), non-recyclable waste! (Not to mention nuclear waste, for example, which borders on astronomical recycling deadlines). In fact, and—I specify:—on the scale of its environment for example, humanity is much less wise than its own ancestors, says: "primitive". And nowhere is this more true than with the famous: three "elephants in the room":

1) An unbridled and unsustainable proliferation of our human population on the planet where we live;
2) Our absurd stubbornness about infinite progress and unlimited economic growth;
3) The civilian and military nuclear power.

The first two "elephants"—our proliferation and unbridled progress / growth—have the potential to eliminate humans by "smothering" them in their own waste of civilization. And the third "elephant"—nuclear in general—simply has the power to extinguish almost any life at any moment of their disruption or explosion (a world breakdown of three days in electricity would be enough!).
These are rather "cumbersome" perspectives. It's the least we can say.
Thus, despite our "great advantage" of being relatively conscious humans, we see that the problem, the sadness and the tragedy of the human condition, particularly pronounced among city dwellers, come largely from the loss of our emotional bonds with other living beings, including other human beings, with our links to the Earth and its organic or inorganic

components. And further with the great Universe itself, its cycles and laws.
In other words: By losing our respect, our love, and our empathy, we lose our natural attachment of the "wize" with the Universe (not to be confused with the "good"). In the true sense: we do not recognize it anymore.

Of course, some people believe this is not very important. But observe this feeling of happiness that invades us when we give or receive a simple gesture of kindness, when we cuddle a pet or stroke a horse, when we smell a flower or see koi in a pond, when we walk on pine needles in a forest, when we gaze with wonder at the colours of autumn leaves, at sunrise or at undulating hills in early morning mist. And, when we find we have a new friend or "suddenly" fall in love. At such moments, life suddenly seems like "magic"— what we call in the social sciences "the love affect"— and everyone, even the most insensitive of humans, has experienced it in one way or another at least once since birth.

So, yes, we are no longer one with the Universe but, from time to time, we are exhilarated by a renewal of sublime contact sublime contact with the univers! There is therefore a sense of truth in us in this "wise" affect. And it is a sense of truth that is included in the depths of life in general (plants that appreciate Mozard, like cuddly animals, experience the same sense of "what is good for them") .! Remember how, when O Sensei went to Ayabe with the Omoto sect, to develop "ki" and achieve peace and harmony, he often went into the hills to practice misogi purification of the body in mountain lakes and streams. And in Iwama, even though there was war, did not agriculture take over? Surely this was communion with nature and the Universe, big time!

So, how can we recover this affect of "good" in our life, this unconditional respect, this pointless love of everything and everyone? "How to restart it"?

Well, our disintegration was not done in a day: so our reintegration will not happen in a day either. As we say, a journey of a thousand miles always starts with one step forward. So all the news is not "doom and gloom". So for even a demiurge, especially a demiurge, each one of us can and must make a start and, with that first step, begin to relearn ways of living in more coherent directions with this natural sense of life.

However, to relearn this true value of life, there are, of course, several ways to do it. One of these "Tantras*" is fairly well defined by the practice and philosophy of the founder's Aikido. Because one of the roles of Aikido is to help us get moving, healthy, refocus, and reconnect with the Universe. Hence the importance in Aikido of the concepts of non-belligerence, or non-enemy, non-competition or non-rivalry. And hence the importance of this idea of "Spirit of love". Which means precisely: the integration / taking into account of our surroundings and our environment, certainly, but more widely of the world, of its needs, and of all its beings. And this allows us to become again and again the animators, protectors and guardians, even and especially socially speaking.

Tantra / Tantrism (from the Sanskrit word "devanagari"), which literally means: the weft of a tissue, and in the figurative sense: the rule of liberation, the metaphysical treatise, here taken in its general sense: Set of texts, doctrines, rituals, or initiation methods of re-awareness of Man in the world.

In Japan, this philosophical trait of willingness to study one's own life is named with honorary deference a "shugyo"(修行), meaning also the sort of ascetic practice that is deep mind-body training. In this case, that is to say, "the search for our essence through spontaneous and intentional confrontation with changes in contradictory contingencies that are internal to us"—a kind of ascetic practice, which everyone can, in everyday life, perform—. Aikido's role is to stimulate this search—a kind of ascetic practice—with, as a special study reference, the Aiki concept of permanent adjustment of In and Yo with each other. And this search support is "personalized" by the dynamic and aggressive action of a "model" partner—namely an "attacker"—and he is for Aikido-ka, as in an old-fashioned photographic laboratory: "the revealer"—.

It is on this theme of the confrontation seen by the Aiki, a confrontation at the beginning quite practical, physiological, dynamic, and martial, that emerges mainly and following logic, so by the Aikido that we practice, this refocusing: this double integration. And so: his active philosophy and his pragmatic pacifism (or "should emerge" because it was—or was not—always the case, far from it).

As you can see, "The philosophy of Aikido" is not easy to tackle an issue in a few lines. Already, it must be said that it is a kind of "culture" in its own right—a culture with a very universalist tendency, but one surrounded by a halo of japanese hermeticism or veiling. In fact, "mystery, enigma, disorder, halo, fog …" are words that come to the Western mind that seeks to think Aikido.

And just by saying that, one doesn't really get rid of the problem of knowing exactly what this philosophy is. For example, John Stevens, whose publisher titled one of his books The Philosophy of Aikido (Kodansha Int., 2001), sets out his work into chapters with titles such as Fundamental Principles, Nature and Health, Tantra, Art, and Aikido and Society!

In this way, we can clearly see it's not really a question of philosophy, but rather—and quite correctly—some of perspectives that I will come back later. It's a little annoying, because in this case it "drowns the fish".

Continuing on, the philosophy of Aikido is closely linked to the two quasi-contradictiory experiential and historical extremes. Firstly, the experiential formation of Aikido by its founder. This experience is typically Japanese in that it was linked to the ancient ancestral chronicles of Japan, the Kojiki, which we will look at later. They are so typically mystical—almost timeless—that they were hardly comprehensible to the Japanese themselves. In fact, Morihei Ueshiba's texts are difficult for modern Japanese to read in their original versions. Indeed, Aikido's formation is characterized by the way Morihei Ueshiba understood or grasped the world "with his hand".

Secondly, Morihei Ueshiba's successors' attempts to justify their policy regarding Aikido's international popularization and its role as a sporting or relaxation activity. That policy really was literally a kind of "creation of a new territory". But these views were already outlined by the founder just after the end of the war and started with the official registry of the word "Aikido" with the Ministry of Health and Welfare—This was probably done under the influence of Butoku Kai*—and then, as we'll see, more methodical over time after his death.

* "I know that the art was called "Aikido" during the war under the influence of the Butokukai" (Interview with Tokimune Takeda (AikiNews #88). Dai Nippon Butoku Kai: a Japanese association and one that is very influential in traditional budo).

So, past this quasi-neutral praxis of our dual integration, we see here that one new extreme of thought wants to "pull the cover of Aikido for its own use": Materialism, which is the new great sect of the world. And, now, it is already very clear that, sooner or later, these antinomic conceptions within the Aiki: Spirituality and Materialism, would lead to a kind of catch-22 situation.

A DIFFICULT INTELLECTUAL DILEMMA

- Even today, Aikido comes up against the obvious problem of the conceptual dilemma inherent in its formation. The recent meeting of the International Federation (IFA) in Tanabe (Japan, 2008) has clearly shown that high-level leaders in global Aikido can't agree on a clear conceptualization of what defines Aikido. And therefore on an effective worldwide coordination on the ethical and ontological positioning of this art.

This is hardly surprising since the experts work with disjointed approaches which are themselves too often in opposition. Hence these irrevocable differences: traditionalism versus modernism; aspiration against moralization; ancestral wisdom versus educational sportsmanship; obstinacy versus openness, non-violence and non-competition against violence and competition; history versus modernity, pedagogy versus transmission, and so on. ~~The dual list would be long~~.

The work of enlightenment, if any, is done in a way that is absolutely confusing, in fits and starts, confused, and "blind". Above all, the work is done quite imprecisely, and Japan's dislike of Western-style "reasoned" social science doesn't help matters either. Nor does its way of preventing any possible critical spirit or upward rise of any thought or reflections within the various administrative hierarchies—an approach the Japanese society always puts in place to protect its leaders and its pyramidal system.

And, even if this social way of doing things guarantees the continuation of a kind of "Japanese historical hegemony" over the art within Japan itself, they still remain completely ossifying today.

In this way, at the end of this or that discourse, we find a little bit of everything about the philosophy of Aikido but above all—to tell the truth—not a great deal of philosophy. That is to say, we are some witness to essences or principles, values or ideas, perspectives or probabilities, flashes of opinions or guiding notions, certainties or "voicing of opinions", stereotypes or conventional frameworks and conceptual collages. And all of these without really trying to understand what it's really all about at the fundamental level.

WHAT, THERE'S A LINK TO PHILOSOPHY?

- Overall, then, what does one find in place of a real philosophical concept, one that is clearly and duly described? A set of vague "catch-all" observations. Year after year, they are drawn from or associated with doctrines or historical reflections related to the foundation of Aikido, its history, Eastern culture, Aikido's later modernist development, various Western sociologies, or even "bar conversations". So it is that we find—blended under the term "Philosophy of Aikido" and looking like a bizarre "hotchpotch" worthy of *Alice in Wonderland*, the following assorted rumblings:

- Dynamic philosophy centreed on harmony;

- Dynamic philosophy centreed on peace;

- Dynamic philosophy centreed on the spiritual force;

- Seek to dissuade the adversary rather than to defeat him;

- Use the strength of the opponent to control him;

- Harmonization of man with his environment;

- Philosophy of Peace and peaceful resolution of conflicts;*

- Harmonization of man with his environment;

- Better understanding of others;

- A philosophy which does not seek to destroy, but to make the adversary aware that continuation of his attack is useless and can only lead him to his own defeat;

- Formative action and even personal development of the individual—action that is educational, pedagogical, civic, physical, moral and so on;

- Social vision of man as part of the universe;

- Mastering an opponent without hurting him;

- Union of one's energy with that of an adversary to divert his attack and use it to one's advantage;

- Emergence of a global culture;

- In Aikido we are invincible because we never fight;

- Opening to the world, and so on.

This notion of «Peace» is a purely an attempt to disconnect from other martial arts. This operation represents a real challenge for Aikido since it' amounts to a feud or quarrel with other martial arts into the bargain, and thus—paradoxically—a war philosophy
.

So obviously, faced with all these incongrous general ideas—*admittedly and, as we will see, not devoid of sense but, in fact, devoid of "real determining points"*, there is only one answer. This is, of course, the most simple and the best answer—one that really upsets no one—and it consists of saying, as do many masters or shihans who don't want to "get wet" on an intellectual level, "... that the philosophy of Aikido is found in its practice, within his practice. So, instead of discussing its philosophy—or heaven knows what else that nobody really understands in Aikido—we have to—and it's more than enough—to practice"!

In short here: "Forget any consideration of actually thinking, become intellectually about as relevant as a mussel but—unlike the so-called molusc—sweat and you'll see...".

The idea that "it will come while training" originally comes from a tantric interpretation of Aikido which says that "the action is at the beginning of the way" (J. Stevens). And that the body—previously purified by misogi, kokyu-ho breathing exercises, or their practice in Aikido—is the "vehicle" of action in Aikido and therefore implicitly the teaching vehicle of its philosophy.

In *The Spritual Fondations of Aikido* (1995), William Gleason speaks of "the practice (as) being the tool of the study of the principle", and this, in my own opinion, is absolutely correct. Just the same, it's a bit of a sneaky way to dodge the philosophical problem before it actually arises. And this, even if Aikido is indeed what we can really call "A Philosophy of Action or Philosophy in Action". However, I have already developed this concept widely in my previous books, and therefore will not come back to it here.

So, all that is very well and good and, while I have to emphasize that it is—by and large—the answer, it still does really move things forward or get us anywhere at all. Mathieu Perona*, a French graduate of the Ecole des Hautes Etudes en Sciences Sociales, Ph.D. in Economics, and practicing in Paris, wrote most intelligently on this very subject. That is to say, he wrote about the problematic of this subject or, in other words, actually defining the problem, the most important step in finding a path towards a viable answer.

He very clearly defines it for Aikido in the following way. "Current Aikido is no longer essentially a Japanese practice. Its dissemination to the four corners of the planet calls for a diversity of styles and encounters with local cultures. But in this diversity, it is for Aikido to not lose its soul. (...) ... beneath the apparent diversity and sometimes the rivalries of styles, *there is only one Aikido*. And it is *this one Aikido* that it's important to defend in its entirety, in a conflict between martial arts values and those of sport in a leisure society."

To read in French if this link is still active on:
http://www.parisaikidoclub.com/spip/spip.php?article60

In the next section, we will further explore his idea which aimed at showing the philosophy of the art or, if you prefer, its soul. The image is, at least in my own opinion, both most appealing and correct.

DISCOURSE THAT STIMULATES -

It has to be said that, if one can easily understand that the "the body and soul" of Aikido is torn between two extremes—traditional martial values and those of sport in a consumer society—an inherent question immediately arises. And that is: "Essentially, fundamentally, what is the unvarying centre, the integral "soul" of Aikido"? This "soul", "this spirit of the many spirits" of Aikido, its "base", its unvarying and intangible centre, this focus of beams, this "hard" and conceptual nucleus of Aikido, this germ, this shared or would-be shared essence, and whatever else I can try to call it here. In short, how can we define it?

Of course it is necessary—at the beginning at least—to look for the beginnings of a definition within the words and actions of the founder of Aikido. Then, it will be interesting to see how this track leads us to a "modern", generalizable, coherent and viable evolution of the original conceptualization. A conceptualisation which has now become barely understandable.

First let's go back a bit. In an old interview formerly published in Japan (Aikido, Kowado, 1957*), Morihei Ueshiba summarized his art in a very concrete and precise way. I was determined to translate this absolutely remarkable text by working long and hard on the original Japanese version. Indeed, the commonly used French translation was apparently only made from an English version which had erased many of the extremely precise nuances of the founder in his own language. So here in a precise English translation of the direct Japanese to French version—one much closer to the original—you will immediately recognize that we are far removed from an innocuous discourse and that each term within it is very important.

*The original version is given in Japanese at the end of the book.

Journalist (B): Aiki is a martial way, but at the same time a teaching in the divine sense. From that, the spirit of Aikido ...

O Sensei: What we call Aiki is, on one hand, "Love"*, our affection (*heart*) seen as the great Love of the Universe ("*heaven and earth*"). This beating "heart" is understood to be the personalization of our mission of assistance towards everything within the Universe, and the true martial way (*shin no bu no michi*) must be the perfect accomplishment of this mission. The warrior of truth (*shin no bu*) vanquishes himself, eliminates the fighting heart of the enemy... no, the notion of the enemy as such disappears completely in the path of unconditional fulfilllment of oneself. Thus the Aiki warrior's technique as bodily experimentation of the laws of heaven, follows the order of the way in the act of reaching the supreme finitude of body-mind unity or, in Japanese, *reiniku-ittai*, meaning "*the soul and body are one*".

*Love: Although the complex Japanese kanji (pictorial character) for love (愛)—thirteen brush strokes—is not the same as the kanji "Ai" (合) in "Aikido", this "Ai" (合)—meaning "joining together"—is often incorrectly translated into French and English as "love". Why the confusion, you might ask. **Well, it's mainly because, when spoken, the two different kanji are pronounced in the same way: they are phonetically the same.** *So different kanj, same pronounciation.*

*For the record, the more complex kanji character for love, in fact, contains within it, the character ukeru (uke) meaning give-receive, >so we can clearly detect (in the pictogram) a sense of "emotional exchange" with a glimmer of hope, aspiration, mobilization and of desire his breast (**heart**)*

*Finally, there is perhaps another reason for the confusion. O Sensei (at a given moment) started to use this phonetic similarity (**same pronounciation**) to make a play on words to introduce the «peace and **love**» notion into Aikido!*

B: Could one then say that Aiki becomes the path that leads to the peace of the world?

O Sensei: Its decisive design is precisely the dawn of a heavenly paradise on earth. In any case, the whole world must come into concordance**. If one acts in this perspective, atomic or hydrogen bombs are rendered useless, and this world becomes a pleasant and agreeable place to live.

***Concordance: The word concordance or concord is expressed in Japanese here by the term "wago", composed of the kanji (pictogram) 和 pronounced **wa** ("peace") and the kanji 合 pronounced **go** (receiving, giving, putting together).*

*Now, as you can see if you check the explanation of Aikido and love above, the kanji character pronounced **go** in wago and the kanji pronounced **Ai** in Aikido are, in fact, **the same simple kanji** 合. So, same meaning (namely, putting together) but different pronounciation.*

*This means that, in Japanese langage, "concord" is the **Ai** of **Aikido** linked with **wa**, peace. So, in Japanese, there's a similar etymology (origin and history) as for English and French, which are based on Latin where con (Latin for with) is linked to cor, genetive cordis (Latin for heart) to arrive at "putting together, putting in sync of hearts".*

*For the record, the kanji **wa** is also used to give a Japanese flavour to other kanji characters: wafu, Japanese way; wabun, Japanese style; and wagokoro, fundamental Japanese soul, the idea of social consensus at any price.*

In spite of the linguistic difficulties inherent in O Sensei's words, upon careful examination, we will find they contain a remarkable density of thought encapsulating profound truths.

DENSITY OF THOUGHT
- Within the very compact text in the preceeding section, as readers will certainly have noticed, there are several very interesting prominent philosophical aspects which are far from easy to understand. With the aim of clarifying our research, they will be discussed in this section, and

are naturally placed in order with a crescendo of meaning.

Firstly, it is "Aiki"—not "Aikido"—that has been equated with "Love" in the original text. That is to say, the "affection of Love", meaning the way the soul—our feeling, if you prefer—is touched or penetrated by the sentiment of Love. In fact, this is a "love affect" or free and energetic exchange of love between oneself and the Universe with no particular object other than the elementary and holistic globality—ourselves included—of the world around us. Here we find the notion of "elementary affective state" of the human being. Moreover, it must be noted—and it is of extreme important here—that this notion of "Aiki" is where the adventure of Aikido, so to speak, began.

As we have seen, "Aiki" is historically the name of the martial technique particular to the "inhabitants of castles" and therefore elitist with a predestined vocation. In other words, this "love" is, on the one hand, equally well a technique and not just anything or emerging out of nothing, and on the other, not just from Morihei Ueshiba's imagination.

Secondly, this "love" is "our affection (*heart*) deemed to be the great love of the universe". Here, there is no repression or channeling of this emotional state, but rather it is taken as an entire vector of our emotional intelligence and personal profile and, therefore, as the foundational basis of our actions. We understand that, according to Morihei's way of thinking, the Aiki we've spoken of here is not some kind of qualifying addition to our essence, but the very verbal expression of our essence.

Thirdly, "Aiki" ... is this "heart" understood to be the personalization of our mission of assistance towards everything". This means, once this emotional state becomes one's intensive and expansive centre (essence), it becomes conscious and comes to envelop our field of perception and, therefore, of our action on our surrounds.

Fourthly, this is a "**mission**". *We will see later on how this notion of mission, while a constant with Ueshiba Morihei, has "changed uniform" over time.* So it is that we are simultaneously "put here" in a position of ontological independence, and in a position of "sending for ...", and of "arrival in order to..." leading to, in a word, ethics. This "being put there who is me" is expressed in the Japanese mantra (*shukaku* 主客) of "the master and the host (at the same time)" of "the principal and the negligible". This mantra of "I am there, between" and "I am all the Universe, microscopic and infinite at the same time (fractal)"—is not associated with an object or a specific objective, but rather with a useful and purposeful direction which fashions an action.

Lastly, "the true martial way (*shin no bu no michi*) must be the perfect accomplishment of this mission" means the action or the goal of this active ontological position consists of finding the truth of the Budo and putting it into practice. Certainly putting it into practice, and if we now have the answer to the question "what?", we still have to know **how** to put it into practice. So the questions of **why, when** and **where also** remain and, as we shall see in the next section, the founder's discourse goes on to respond very clearly to these questions.

ANSWERS WITHIN THE WORDS -

Concerning the "**HOW**", firstly Morihei's phrase "**the warrior of truth (*shin no bu*) vanquishes himself, eliminates the fighting heart of the enemy...**" contains the answer. To overcome—over and above this "self put there in the action of intervening party"— can can be summed up as eliminating the combatitive remnants in one's own heart. One's heart is fighting, aggressive, antagonistic and the emulator of one's own vanity to exist as this or that, and it is the elimination of these (four) remnants which will make it possible to overcome the same traits in the fighting heart of the enemy.

Secondly, the phrase "**No, the notion of the enemy as such disappears completely in the path of unconditional fulfilment of oneself**" is important. This is a clear break from the founder's own reflection—possibly from his own "fighting heart"— and it is a kind of flashback. Or rather a change of plan that this time becomes a pure plan of transcendental reflection: that we must go beyond this idea of fighting hearts. We must even go even further than the very notion of a fighter and "an enemy" or, as Spinoza would have said, "to go from the relation to the essence".

To reinvent the "**HOW**" of the true Budo, it is necessary to go beyond the very notion of "enemy" and replace it with the idea of completeness of the world, of its possible concordances within a completely new perception of it. *This is an articulation of a very important thought by the founder, no doubt the greatest inspiration he had.* And this, because it moves the concept of Budo from a rather vulgar educational idea ("the effects") to a much higher martial arts stage, one that is transcendental, philosophical and ethereal.

And, now let's move on to the "**WHY**". According to J. Stevens, in the phrase "**the Aiki warrior's technique as bodily testing of the laws of heaven…**", we find notions of "misogi", of "kokyu-ho" and purifying practices, and of purification of this "body vehicle". And fromthis comes the very powerful notion of the body as a means of purifying the soul.

The conceptual idea here is one of a philosophical action by a "knowing body", of a philosophy of action and therefore of an "applied philosophy". *A philosophy in action—not only theoretical and intellectual, but also practical and physical—is also a very important and unwavering notion for O Sensei.* It is moreover a very original and unique idea of ancient Japan, which—without one realising it at first glance—very much continues on in modern Japan. In this respect, it is rather like the way Christianity (religion) or Homer's Odyssey (history-literature) can, for example, influence our vision of the world—a vision believed to be a personal, autonomous, or culturally identity, whereas it is obviously not so.

Then we come to the "**WHEN**" and "**the Aiki warrior's technique (as bodily attainment of the laws of heaven) follows the order of the way in the act of reaching the supreme finitude of body-mind unity**." In Japanese this is *reiniku-ittaika* (霊肉一体化), and it means "*the soul and body become one*" or simply, integration.

This "heavenly peace" arising from the practice of Aikido, is an allusion to an advanced state of the self that will "become the universe" or which will once again identify with the universe. So it's a time-related evolutionary process of becoming of "non-anomaly" of oneself. And this, not only through essence, but also by perfection of an ontological placement from every point of view, in both the material world (its great particularity here) and the spiritual world. In this way, placement becomes ideal, energetic, ethical, social, religious, cultural, relational, and naturally moral. In fact, the morality is literally "ejected" from the very idea of Aiki, even if it remains strong and socializationing in the idea of the Do. Placement is then, for the founder, an active state, reactive, and creator of peace or, in a word, "divine"—absolute and eternal through perpetual regeneration.

It is the state of absolute creative purification or, what is called in Japan, the divine technique of "Odo". And, according to his calligraphy master, Seiseki Abe Sensei, Morihei Ueshiba sought this all his life. I would quote this master here: "According to the Kojiki (the Japanese book of ancient things, dating from 712

AD), after Izanami-no-Mikoto (the original female deity, often referred to as the Japanese goddess of creation) escaped the world of death, she practiced a ritual purification near the Odo or, in Japanese, "source of the river". When she had purged herself of impurities, some kami ("divinities") were born. Then, when she entered the water and purified herself, more kami were born. O Sensei said that Aikido was born from the blows of Izanagi-no-Mikoto (the original male deity called "the inviting male", creator of the Sun and the Moon) during her purification. From my point of view, O Sensei's whole life search was essentially the search for Odo's divine techniques". (Aikido Journal, No. 114, 1998).

If I were to translate and decode Seiseki Abe's words, I believe they would mean the founder's research was centred on the phenomenon of the birth of the gods, through the interaction of male and female agents. Of course, it must be understood that the word "gods" here not only has a "pantheistic" meaning, but above all a very general and animistic sense—the Shinto sense—of "divinities" as being beyond our earth-bound materiality.

And finally, we come to the question of "**WHERE**" and the answer lies in O Sensei's words, "**Its (Aiki's) decisive design is precisely the dawn of a heavenly paradise on earth**". This means that *purification in the union of opposites is the means of arriving at "creation"*. In looking at the full interview with the founder of Aikido, it can be seen (dramatically) that his vocabulary vigorously moves from the notion of "interpretation" to that of the "spirit" in Aikido. In this way, he situates two major stages in Aikido thinking, aiming at their integration and appropriation. And so it is that he migrates the thinking about the interpretation of "The Three Victories"—Masakatsu, the "authentic victory", Agatsu, the "victory of our mission", and Kawatsuayabi, the "instant victory"—to the notion of the spirit of "peace".

And this may leave us somewhat perplexed. Yet it is this subtle difference that makes for all the richness in his thinking. The fact is he doesn't just provide us with a new version or a new value of the notion of victory, he directly transfers the meaning of the word "victory" to a plane of immanence. *Here, it's not the victory of "I want to win" while being the victory of "I've already won" and, as a result, the word "victory" no longer makes sense and becomes almost rediculous.* Thus the only advantageous thing to do is to replace it by another word—"peace"—and this finally and historically brings to a close the "victories" debate which, thanks to Aikido, and without doubt for O Sensei, is rendered sterile.

We have seen how Morihei Ueshiba said, "**In any case, the whole world must come into concordance**". It is in his interview that the word "concordance" first makes its appearance. It is clearly stated and in Japanese this time: *wago* or "concord". Effectively, he suggests—possibly assumes—a phasing (putting in sync) of the parts which form us with the **All**. There is the task of "the duty of concordance" to perform (*shina kereba naranai:* しなければならない), and it's a necessity, a need, and an **imperative of concordance** that he clearly expresses here.

Contrary to what many people thought when they first read my book *Understanding Aikido*, while I used the term for a better understanding of Aikido, it certainly wasn't me who invented the wonderful concept of "<u>**concordance**</u>". As can be seen without a shadow of a doubt from the following lines in Japanese, it was the founder of Aikido, Morihei Ueshiba—and before him the historical lineage of teachers of the real "Aiki" who used it first.

Referring to the "duty of concordance", he said, "If we act in this perspective" (*so sureba*), this duty is not impersonal, virtual or purely theoretical, it is a goal towards which we ourselves must strive. This concordance is what we must achieve in ourselves and therefore "in the world". And he went on to say, "atomic or hydrogen bombs are rendered useless, and this world becomes a pleasant and agreeable place to live". It is surely the uselessness of the enemy and thus the uselessness of a defense and even the notion of deterrence of the enemy, that must be achieved.

Here we witness the disappearance of these very ideas since they have become obsolete and useless. And for the founder, this disappearance is synonymous with a world of peace in which it finally becomes possible to "live well"—*sumi yoi* in Japanese—and, in fact, a pleasant world (*tanoshii sekai*).

So we see that, in return for this meteoric progression

of thought, extremely luminous, the whole question of immanence (the true nature of things) now arises in Aikido.

IMMANENCE: A UNIVERSAL PRESENCE
- In thinking about immanence, we must ask ourselves in what exactly, is there in Aikido this creation of "peace"? And even, what is it then fundamentally, philosophically speaking, about this "peace"—a peace so absolute and perfect—that redefines and shapes "a pleasant world"?

Aikido is certainly not—as we rather like to say so simply—the art of "making or not making war". And Morihei Ueshiba's about-turn during his interview clearly shows that we have to "break this old argumentative plaything of war or animal superiority". In fact, we must move on to another age—an age of Man with a capital "M"—and another stage of thought, in a way, becoming "Adult".

It is rather a matter of moving the goal of the art—and therefore this "victory through peace"—onto a plane other than that of the war-peace opposition: that of a real "intensity" of life... without war "within" oneself. There is here more than simply the idea of a sort of pact with "**life**"—life both material and immaterial, both spiritual and reasoned (possibly resonant), both original (birth) and ultimate (death), and constructive. There is the idea that this very act—the pact—will simultaneously "fix" and liberate the world around us, withdrawing war itself from this world because, even at the primitive level, war simply no longer makes any sense.

WHAT IS THE AIKIDO PACT?
- We already know that it's a pact of "concordance" with the constituent elements of the world, but I'm going to come back to it here since the concept is sufficiently powerful and very clearly stated in the interview text. In fact, as I have already said, it (the pact) may well clearly define Aikido in an autogenic or self-generating way. For this notion, please refer to my book *Understanding Aikido* (Budo Edition, 2nd edition, 2007) which unveils this univocal concept of Aikido, and demonstrates its relevance.

I believe it's very important to understand that—far, far from the ancient Greek philosophy of Plato—the Aikido pact is one of "intimacy". By this I mean very far from Plato's philosophical necessity of rivalry or from the importance he ascribes to pretension, and therefore very far from the Platonic necessity of a "generalized athleticism". Moreover, very far from ***agon***, the ancient Greek term for a struggle or contest in sports or even in the classical theatrical debate of opposition or contradiction.

However, Aikido's "all-encompassing" intimacy goes beyond a sense of comfort or of simple "pleasure" to become a truly intimate thing: an "emotional, active, and constructive fusion with the world". And, as I believe, one can go as far as saying that this "intimacy"—potentially speaking—becomes a constitutive fusion of the world, of "a new world".

THE NOTION OF INTIMA - This
"fusion" of oneself, this origin, this secret, this "intima"—the essential intimate matrix of the world in us—does not move, by the operation of Aiki, to the state "outside of us" just to be devoured. It's not exactly a question of a predatory act here. The intimate in us does not turn inside out like a giant sock on the world and aggression to become like a flesh-eating envelope for them. Quite the contrary, this "Intimate"—through the operation of Aiki—turns into a "supra-state" with everything that penetrates or infiltrates it. It ends up integrating and becoming one with all that penetrates it—note the ech of the *irimi* concept here—forming "something else" or "another state", quite different from the first. In other words, a new or "second identity" that marks—like a living and moving puzzle constantly changing the final image—the completeness of the world or "worlds" enclosed and intertwined with one another. And, as in the In-Yo—Taoist concept of unique in the One—it is this completeness that is also a part in us.

At this point, we come back to—yes, we recognize—a very **tantric** idea of Aikido, that is to say, the notion of a reconciliation between "the act of love of Aikido" and, for example, a carnal act between man and woman having a transcendental vocation. It is also here that we recognize the idea of Kotodama—father and mother sounds—whose harmonics are the result of the same echoes of mutual interphasing. Of course, it's understood here that it's the same word "love" that creates the bond, and it means the same thing every time—in theory as in practice, in the virtual and spiritual as in reality and the material. Yes, the same thing, but only if the word "love" and the word "sexual" are understood as being processes of changes and transformations and of expansion of the vital awareness and "intimate of the world". And not as dualist—or separate—versions of consciousnesses forced into competition, but rather as condordance.

CONCORDANCE - As a start, it's important to attempt to find a fairly simple explanation of what this word actually means. Take, for example, "the intimate concord in all things" for "X". We have in this process two subjects, "X" and "Y" which, by expanding one into the other—contact-relation—form a third, "Z". In this union, the world of "X" and the world of "Y" are mixed in a way that is unique to them both.

"X" becomes concordant with "Y", for example, if he or she accepts and onboard the fact that he or she is the very set of all the "Zs" possible with "Y" at the moment of their fusional meeting... but without believing itself to be only an "X".

In this way, we see that "concord" or "intimacy" here do not represent processes of appropriation (predation), nor are they either processes of possessions or objectification. They are, in fact, processes of exchange and multiplication which, by the way, is not necessarily egalitarian.

The penetration act—irimi and atemi in Aikido—while sexual in some tantric practices, synchronization in kotodama, and recognition of double layers in all things in astrophysics—isn't the attainment of monopolisation or usage. Rather it's the fulfilment of a supra-ontological "expansive diffusion"—both positive and negative—in perpetual, moving symbiosis, complementary and harmonic. And, in the case of "X" and "Y", this expansive diffusion can neither be defined by "X" alone nor by "Y" alone, but can always be defined by the many possible "Zs", themselves shifting in the characteristics of the relationships.

Now let's turn to **In** and **Yo**. In their relationship, the concordance of Aikido is both "intimate" and "intimal", similarly to the physical act of love, although on a different plane of inclusion. This Aiki concordance can only be achieved by a process of revelationary ecstatic inter-relation. Moreover an inter-relation which is both immense—infinitely large, ethereal, volatile, empty and celestial like the **sky**—and, at the same time, microscopic in itself—infinitely small, heavy, massive, material and atomic like the **earth**.

As J. Stevens reminded us, that is why, in this sense Onisaburo Deguchi wrote:

"The concordant* mixture of male and female gives birth to heaven and earth. And the true form of heaven and earth is a couple in a state of ecstatic union"

*Please note that I have replaced the word "harmonious" in his version of the translation by the word "concordant" so that

the reader may better understand the issue that is being cleared up here.

Mankind is at the centre of these two, that is to say he or she is the exact relay of the ecstasy of heaven and that of Earth. And so it is that mankind is, a priori, the concrete manifestation—the point of personified ecstasy itself—of the relationships between Heaven and Earth, the extremes of the world.

The concept of Aikido can therefore be defined by the term "intimate concordance" in the sense of a permanent and ecstatic concordance which is appeasing for the entire world. Aikido is this attempt at absolute integration of the world into mankind and, at the same time, this "intimate concordance" process with "the worlds" that mankind—in his own way—similarly integrates.

Ueshiba Morihei believed that mankind was itself composed of five worlds*, five strata, or layers of itself. It was necessary for man and woman—again by the practice of Aikido—to unite these "strata" in "one", in action and in being.

It is my considered opinion that the influence of Omoto-kyo's universal syncretism on him is rather obvious, and that Morihei Ueshiba's notion of the five bodies of mankind emerges from a learned and heteroclytic mixture. Namely, that of the Kosha concept from India, of the five Buddhist patriarchs, of the five bodies of the pentagram (Judaism, Christendom) and obviously of the bodies of Shinto religion. The latter being **one spirit and **four souls (Ichirei, Shikon)** which are constantly seeking their inter-relational balance from "the worlds" This is the fundamental creed of O Sensei's thinking: balances-fullness-happiness-function. The Shinto "souls" are **Aramitama**, **Nigitama**,*

***Kushimitama**, **Sachimitama** and **Ichirei**. Now we come across these five bodies or "envelopes" of mankind—they're rather like Russian nesting dolls—in other practically similar religious guises around the world. For example, among Buddhists, there are the five "Buddha Patriarchs" ("Goshi-nyorai") who are Akshobya, Amitabha, Amoghasiddhi, Ratnasambhava and Vairocana. These Buddhas themselves designate in our current state the five aggregates: the **forms (body, matter)**, the **sensations (the energetic)**, the **perceptions (the etherial)**, the **mental factors (the mind)** and **consciousness (the astral)**. And it is these five aggregates which determine our spiritual progression on the five paths of **accumulation, junction, vision, meditation,** and **non-study**.*

For the information of the reader—and with the proviso that my knowledge of the subject is rather meager—the five (Shinto) bodies of mankind are listed below.

***Aramitama--Our physical body:** our material fixation (matter) to the other four envelopes on Earth. This is our physiology made of flesh and bone, cellular humors, and circulation of fluids as well as exchanges and subtle molecular chemistry, genetic code and ancestral or hereditary lineage included. They correspond to the Vajra (diamond-lightning) in Vayrayan Buddhism. And here we find the **In** and **Yo** of Aiki, represented by Buddhists by this ~~double~~ object in the form of five prongs and other motifs centreed on a ball or club. In this form of buddhism the five prongs symbolize the five Wisdom Buddhas, of which Akshobya (Ashuku Nyorai: Buddha of the East (associated with the element water) is the embodiment of mirroir knowledge or what is real and what is illusion, and therefore the Buddha of the appeasement of the sufferings and disturbances of the spirit.*

***Nigitama--Our energetic body (vital):** our body of **"Ki"**, our body of electrical lines (nerves) and electromagnetic lines as well as that of meridians, nadis and chakras, corresponding to the lotus in Buddhism. In Buddhism, the Amitabha Buddha (Amida Nyorai) is the Western Buddha, associated with the element fire and* *universal love, who annihilates our need for predation.*

Kushimitama—Our "etherial" body (causal)*: the whole of our thoughts, feelings, wills, dreams, desires,and so on. In other words, all that is abstract within us, but which also builds us. The Buddhism correspondance is the double Vajra or Vajra cross: the Buddha Amoghasiddhi (Fukujoju Nyorai) or the North Buddha (associated with the element wind) and the Buddha of altruism. He offers us the determination to carry out our tasks.*

Sachimitama—Our mental body*: this is "our ethics", our "I", our ability to have a personal and if possible lucid view of the world. The correspondance in Buddhism is the jewel: the Buddha Ratnasambhava (Hosho Nyorai) or Buddha of the South (associated with the element earth) and the Buddha of the "consciousness of essences". He puts an end to our forms of pride and to our false needs of rivalries.*

Ichirei--Our spiritual body (astral)*: "our soul" or "our double". It is the eternal part of us that cooperates with us, but which can't live in our present –just as we physical beings can neither live in our past or our future. In this sense the soul has need of us, of our experimentation and present material creation to ensure its own future. And it is in this ultimate astral layer that is engraved on the sand of our earthly materiality, our matrix of life. The correspondance in Buddhism is (at the wheel) the Buddha Vairocana (Dainichi Nyorai), Buddha of the centre (associated with the element metal) and of emptiness, the character of that which is empty. He is the one who eliminates our fears.*

Aikido is then not just mere mystical chatter—as is often supposed—nor is it a simple gymnastic gesticulation of the body, of thinking, or even a maso-acrobatic artifice, done without prior reflection.

On the contrary and speaking very seriously, in Morihei Ueshiba's whole idea—in its syncretic expansion based on Omoto Neo-Shintoism—there was the principal notion of **all worlds uniting** to reach plenitude or fullness. *Moreover, according to P. Goldsbury, the ceremonies of Aiki-jinja in Iwama are always held today under the aegis of priests affiliated with Omoto-Kyo*.* This is manifested or shown by the evolution of O Sensei's technique over time as well. Here we are referring to a very mysterious tendency—mysterious for us, at least—for him to be able to connect everything around him, notably intentions of deadly attacks or antagonistic forces approaching him or wanting to touch him, wherever it may be. In this way, one could talk about the "five forces"**" to work in Aikido (Shugyo), in correlation with the five bodies of mankind.

**"The Ueshiba family follows Omoto, and the ceremonies which take place at his tomb in Iwama are Omoto". G. Erard, Guillaumeerard.fr – Interview with Peter Goldsbury – Part 2: History of Aikido – 2016. Perhaps after the death of O Sensei and the schism with Takemusu Aikido—along with the break from the Kuki family—the return of the Omoto priests was inevitable. However, I know little or nothing about that.*

***The five forces are: that of the physical body, the strength of our "Ki", the strength of our thoughts, the strength of our consciousness, and finally the strength of our destiny.*

It is then my firm conviction that it's precisely at the time of Morihei Ueshiba's process of **uniting all worlds** that, for Aikido, there was a movement to another critical semantic shift. Notably, *from* "**The way of energy of union**"– Daito-ryu (ethics)–the **personal** will or determination of "I want", "I must" and "I'm going to… " *to* "**The way of union of energies**"– Aikido (ontology)– impersonal determinism, that is to say "The universal law that tells us that... ".

THE DIRECTION OF LIFE - In this way, we see that these two traits—"concordance" and "intimacy"—form an intention of Aikido that is present in all features that make up this art. Their association shows us that there is no concordance without penetration and simultaneous absorption (exchanges), and without a sort of quasi "implosive-explosive-shared-composition" mixture with something of the other, with something of the world, with the heavenly in us, in him, our... and our endlessness.

And, as I previously explained in one of my books, it is this association of "concordance and intimacy" that prevents us from believing that concordance is linked to a desire for voluntary harmony. It's not harmony that is voluntary—which is explicitly targeted—since harmony is deemed to be "preexisting" to everything anyway, *even chaos. War is a striking example of this: for the winner, war is the creator of **harmony**, isn't it. Because **harmony** is just a **"point of view"**, and that's the problem.* However, it must be understood that concordance is not preexisting to everything. And here, what public opinion puts forward about the philosophy of Aikido (which we quoted previously)—these "rumors" and these "perspectives"—don't don't even remotely define Aikido's central concept that I just mentioned. These rumors, as I called them, are actually poorly understood or poorly maintained components of the concept. They are simple results—often superficial but sometimes less so, of course—of the effects of Aikido's "intimate concordance". Which is, of course, very different too.

In fact, Aikido lays out—sets up, if you like—a new plan of life for mankind, a project of life, a new human and relational cartography. But not only to mankind as part of the world, but conversely—and this is very interesting and cutting edge—it also draws up a plan for "worlds" as a participative element of mankind.

In this, Aikido builds a new problematic, a questioning that is thrown in front of us as human beings. And one naturally asks if this problematic has its roots in a long-forgotten entity. Could it arise from the influence of the Omoto religion? Or perhaps that of the biologist and ecology polymath Kumagusu Minataka (1867-1941)?

In summary then. The Latin philosophical proposition "Cogito ergo sum" from Descartes—"I think, therefore I am" goes right out the window the moment we withdraw the notion of competition or comparison—the terrible Greek idea of struggle (*agon*) against which Ueshiba mounts a revolution. Rather, the question becomes: "How can one finally redefine the notion of "I" in Aikido since this "I" disappears—or is almost wiped out or obscured—faced with the "situational us" in practice, at any rate, from the entrance up to kime"?

In the entire history of philosophy—at least as far as we in the Christian West (especially European) have been privy to—there have been few philosphical projects as profoundly interesting as this. Of course, the Anglo-Saxons were much more advanced in this type of reflection, in history, in philosophy, or in literature at least. As Peter Goldsbury delights in saying, there was the philosophical parallel of Wittgenstein, but it would be long to explain here.

So it is that one suddenly emerges from the realm of the art and science of Aiki bodies to enter the field of philosophy. Or at least to broach the idea that we can put back on the table and open up to discussion the basis of our way of thinking about the world. To think about it—and about us—precisely and "in another way".

>In any event, the upshot is we are no longer speculating on perceptions—at any rate, not only on them—nor only on affects (elemental emotional status, thus arts), nor even on perspectives (sciences) or conversely on judgments (doxa). We are speculating on the essential and existential raw material of us, and this, in a new direction or meaning given to life. And perhaps one might even say that we're talking about, perhaps, a philosophy?

IN A WORD, THE PHILOSOPHY OF AIKIDO

- Let me start by stating quite clearly that there is unquestionably a philosophy of Aikido that can be defined today. This philosophy is engendered—fathered, if you prefer—by the concept of "**concord intima**" or as Morihei Ueshiba said, "from bone to bone". But, as we have seen, it's a clearly definable central concept ("soul"), and one that is, at least as far as I know, unique to this martial art.

In this way, the question of a philosophy of Aikido now largely exceeds the order of its founder's biography to the extent that it can effectively be "depersonalized" from him. We can thus, based on the foundational ideas >he provided us, take it up for ourselves, and manipulate it, expand it and certainly extend it. And this, all the while keeping its "pedigree", as is done for any great nominative philosophy, for that matter.

So, far from being a kind of redundant or superfluous idea, this concept represents the quasi autonomy of Aikido thinking. In any case, that's true when compared to classical martiality or our consumerist values. And, equally well, in relation to the all-powerful Platonic philosophy it deliberately abandoned, because—at a given moment—competition is itself outdated. Moreover, as we will see, this is exactly what happened in the history of Aikido, a story that, in its own way, in an unchanging reflection of it, is similar to the great "History" of the world.

So, of course, like any new concept, it greatly bothers some people—genre, "Above all, let's not look too far"—while finally giving hope to others, genre, "And if there really was genius in all that?" With the "in all that"—by implication—being in Aikido.

POLITICAL AMNESIA! - In this section, we will explore a bit of history or, at least, history as a trigger and a catalyst for the birth of the philosophy we have entitled Aikido. But look out, all this philosophy is not without guile, in the sense that it is something of a political construction of the times. Of course, as we have seen, while "the times" was quite long ago, this is also true for more recent, even quite contemporary times!

In this way, the philosophy of Aikido had its historical mainstays—serving as sources for us—as well as its historical achievements which were "triggers" of its evolution. Now we realize these mainstays and achievements were all very active, notably in Aikido history's players' unique individual and personal temperospatial moments in Japanese history. And, when we say history, we're talking about the socio-cultural, typically Japanese political atmosphere in which these players lived since it was only after 1955 that Aikido really only emerged from its insular chrysalis.

Right from the start when I first began the study of Aikido more than forty years ago in France—later in Japan—I always had the gut feeling there was a mystery to it. I sensed that there were very important unspoken aspects to this extremely enigmatic art. In fact, I saw two main "fault lines"—enigmas, if you prefer—in Aikido that were taboo, and I will describe them.

The first was a **technical taboo** at the very heart of

Aikido. None of all the masters I was close to could teach or even clearly explain to me O Sensei's technique so I could do what one sees in his films, photographs, and so on. For a very long time, this obvious deficiency was, despite my efforts, both very mysterious and very confusing for me.

And the second was a kind of **"semantic" taboo**. I couldn't understand the relationship between the Aikido of competition I was taught—genre *after all, there too, you've got to win, haven't you?*—and the message of peace and the harmony its founder supposedly left for posterity. Somehow they really did not fit. It was playful, enjoyable, strong, skillful and powerful—anything you want, in fact—but no, the initial assumptions and end results just didn't did not fit together at all.

This first enigma was cleared up for me when I began to study the history of Aikido movements by learning Daito-ryu. After all, I realized there had been a technical "changeover" between what the founder did until the end of his life, and what his students did with his teaching or his memory. Yes, there in one shot, everything became very clear. Of course, I now know that it would be incorrect to believe he radically changed his technique after the war. In fact, while it certainly evolved constantly, it didn't change in its principles. The fact is Morihei Ueshiba stuck to the fundamentals of Daito-ryu all his life, and this is absolutely unmistakable for anyone with sufficient knowledge of Daito-ryu!

Quite simply, in the later stages of O Sensei's Aikido, the activation points of Aiki movements kind of "jump" in the eyes of the uninitiated observer: we don't see them any more. The fact was that, at the end of his life, Ueshiba had so melted them into his technique that these points had become invisible. Except that is for his uke because these activation points—extremely condensed by this time and therefore minimalist—well and truly stayed. This realization leaped out at me like a champagne cork, and you can imagine my joy at finally understanding the evolution between the old Aiki and the "modern" Aikido! However, this did not solve the question of "Why". Why this shift between O Sensei's form and that of his followers? And again, a cascade of other questions: Why? Where? When? What? And how ? But I will come back to them later.

The first taboo—the technical one—was largely laid bare: while O Sensei certainly practiced Daito-ryu up until the end of his life, he didn't teach it as such after the end of the war because no one—or nearly no one—could correctly or faithfully imitate him. The primary taboo was first to hide this fact from the students and, secondly, to hide this fact from students later.

So, even if I put my five all-important questions aside for "another day," I still banged my head against the second taboo—the semantic one—or what I will now call the "Gordian-knot* taboo", namely the history of Aikido and its paradoxical "philosophy".

What was the relationship between the Aikido of

competition (martial art, suuposedly *par excellence*) taught all over the world, in Japan too, and the message of peace and harmony also proclaimed worldwide in the name of Morihei Ueshiba? When you think about it, it's quite incredible, isn't it?

*For readers unfamiliar with ancient history, the Gordion knot was an intricate knot so tightly entangled it was impossible to see how to unravel it. Legend had it that the person who managed to untie it would be ruler of all Asia. When Alexander the Great arrived, after trying unsuccessfully to untie it, he cut it in half with his sword, reasoning that **it didn't matter how** it was loosened. Since then, it has been used as a metaphor for solving an intractable problem by creative thinking or, as we would say today, " thinking outside of the box". It is also viewed as being symbolic of daring or flair but, **in any interpretation, there is the shadow of suspicion that, by not doing something correctly, the result is not entirely valid or will not endure***

In any event, to solve this unmanageable mystery, I came up with and constructed many hypotheses, and I read many others who wanted to reconcile the irreconcilable. But nothing really seemed to me to be coherent or clear: I was absolutely not looking for justifications, but answers.

In my way of thinking, "competition and peace" , if not to arm oneself with an intellectual parabellum carved in a very slippery block of black soap, it was certainly like a jigsaw puzzle where two key supposedly-interlocking pieces don't fit together at all. So I turned the problem around in my head and my practice never stopped. Until one day I said to myself, "But finally, what is a taboo?

So it was back to square one and the need to clearly establish some definitions, and firstly that of a taboo.

A **taboo** is *originally* a kind of prohibition pronounced by priests or chiefs in Polynesia, on a place, on an object, on a person, or on talking about something. It is therefore a religious or ritual prohibition, in other words, it is "What we do not even have to see, or even just point out". However, since that time, the object of the prohibition has itself become known as a taboo.

If it is clear there was a **technical shift** of O Sensei's ancestral Daito-ryu in what has been called "Aikido" from 1942 until today, there is inevitably a relationship between this shift and the **semantic taboo**, the second enigma, in fact. Effectively, there's always a direct link between what we do—**how** *we do it and the technique employed*—and the **why** we do it that particular way. *In other words, the idea we have of the thing to be done or, to put it very clearly, its ideology.*

Now we know roughly when this shift occurred—it was between 1942 and 1945 or possibly 1946-1948—but the real question is what exactly happened during this very tight schedule of two to three years for such a change to take place, and therefore so rapidly? And it was in Morihei Ueshiba's account (*his biography* and personal history of Aikido*) and from Japanese and international history with a big "H", that we had to look for answers to this question.

*"Kisshomaru Ueshiba uses his biography [the one in which he writes about his father] to achieve a particular end, namely, to record the

transformation of Aikido into an art that is practiced in a worldwide network of organizations. This biography—superficially the record of "just one f**king thing after another" but mainly concerning one spectacular individual [M.Ueshiba]--becomes a vehicle for Kisshomaru to present his own view of the development of Aikido as a martial art. This presentation is done in a rather subtle way, such that the average reader might not suspect that the biography of his father is really the vehicle for an account of the early years of the evolution of an art now practiced worldwide in what is called "organizations". But it is an account seen through the eyes of the son and heir, and an evolution of facts of which the subject of the biography [his father] might not have been fully aware or have fully approved." (Peter Goldsbury, Transmission / Inheritance / Emulation # 28, XV : Aikido and Organizations – Logic of Dojos: from Kobukan to Aikikai/IAF.

Except for a few specialized historians and the few practitioners passionate about history—actually, there are more of them than we think in the world—for Westerners like us, excluding the main lines of the Pacific war learned at school (almost nothing), this period of Japan's history, say between 1915 and 1942, then 1955, is as clear as black peat. But let's stand back somewhat and try to focus our spotlight a little closer, at least on our enigma.

ALARMING PHILOSOPHICAL PRETENSIONS - In focussing on the "pre-1942" social and political ambiance, I would like begin by citing a very edifying text, taken from an article published in Budo, the magazine of the "Dai Nippon Budo Senyokai*". This was the "Society for the Promotion of Martial Arts", of which Ueshiba Morihei was Chairman from 1932, and which was an organ of the Omoto-kyo sect of Reverend Deguchi Onisaburo. And the magazine article clearly demonstrates the ins and outs of the idea of Budo in pre-war Japan. Now, we must understand—and it is here that we touch on the beginning of a solution for our enigma—that these ins and outs paradoxically formed, make no mistake about it, the true primary ideological ground of the future Aikido philosophy. In fact, it's here the taboo starts to literally crack in front of our eyes. So hold onto your hat since—even if the damning text is dated (1932)—its alarming pretensions are likely to be hard for you to swallow.

"... the true task of Japanese martial arts is to become the leader of all the martial arts on Earth as part of the continuing process of realizing an Imperial Way [Kodo] for the whole world. Japan is the suzerain of the globe, the model for the Earth and the will of the entire world is Greater Japan. Japan is the model form for the perfect world. It is only after this spirit is completely understood/assimilated** that one can really understand the true meaning of Japanese martial arts."

(Text discovered by Peter Goldsbury and published in Transmission-Inheritance-Emulation # 9 – INTERLUDE III: Deguchi, Ueshiba and Omoto, Part 2: The Second Suppression: - The Sakurakai Assassins and Morihei Ueshiba, by Peter Goldsbury).

"I think that O Sensei had a more complex attitude to organizations (...). In 1932, he became Chairman of the Dai

Nippon Budo Senyokai at the request of Onisaburo Deguchi, who was the President. As you know, the main dojo for the Omoto organization was at Takeda, in Hyogo Prefecture, and it appears to have been run as a farm-dojo—growers and farmers—rather like Iwama later became. There appear to have been two dojos and members of the public (presumably Omoto believers) were able to train. When he wasn't there himself, the instructors were Ueshiba's uchi-deshi, most of whom had no links with Omoto.

I do not think the creation of the Zaidan Houjin Kobukai in 1940 was synonymous with the opening of Aiki-budo to the general public." (Peter Goldsbury, Transmission-Inheritance-Emulation # 28, Forum)

So it was that, in Japan of 1932—in the martial arts milieu of Ueshiba Morihei and at the centre of power, Tokyo—a new concept of Budo arose. This was the notion of Budo as a process leading to the perfect Man in a perfect world. Both can only be perfect, so the Budo can only be produced and lived as emanating from "the great Imperial militarist Japan" of that time.*

* *Despite their (the Americans) inability to properly manage the Japanese administration during their occupation—the problem was how to replace the Japanese officials, themselves competent, certainly, but a product of the war and ultra pre-war education—we understand here that the Americans after the Pacific War had very clearly grasped and understood the problem of Japanese militarist, ethnocentric and expansionist thought. We can only respect them for this lucidity. And we also better understand their concerns during the political and social management of the country after the surrender of Japan until the nineteen-fifties.*

Thus, it would be most unwise to turn a blind eye to one very important fact. This rather scary historical environment—*historically cruel and one imbued with a completely psychotic reworking of the Japanese elite's (military) vision of the world, notable fanatical ethnocentrism*—was also the active catalyst in the formation of the entire philosophy of today's Aikido. And this, passing from the audacious Meiji era to the martial law of unbridled militarism—educational, militant extremist, schizophrenic, and ultra-violent—of the pre-Pacific war, notably 1920 to 1942... until the Japanese capitulation. A capitulation which, it must be said, was—in the true sense of the word—a grea trauma for the Japanese people in the twentieth century. And one that remains so up until today.

Nonetheless, while not wanting to downplay the rôle of militarism in the formation of Aikido, we must not only remember that it's only a tool, but also bear in mind that, like most tools and technology, militarism can have dual use.

A TOOL, NEVERTHELESS - Whatever the tool, it doesn't have an inherent negative or positive value in and of itself, but its value is a direct function of what one chooses to do with it, in other words, its vocation.

It must be understood that Japan at that time was, in the eyes of the Japanese—as clearly stated in the magazine article—the centre of the world. In fact, as early as 1853, once forcibly opened to the outside by Commodore Perry, suddenly, this country 'Japan' was becoming unlimited, gigantic for the Japanese. The whole planet in its global immensity had become 'Japan around them, and they the centre of the world', they who had just discovered it with dismay. Obviously two hundred and fifty years of absolute protectionism had something to do with it!

It was quite like that for us Westerners in the fifteenth to nineteenth century with our imperialist expression "*The Colonies*". *And since it even remains so today in Africa, we are hardly in a position to preach to other countries.* The Japanese said to themselves, "But it's about us too, it's us, it's up to us, to us, to us, to us... What a extraordinary windfall of knowledge—science, science, energy, raw materials, land, people, industries, outside labor, and so on! We'll have to reshape all this in our image—an absolutely vertical hierarchical image, so very typical of Japan!"

And that's the principal source of the Japanese imperialistic attitude towards Asia—extremely predatory, violent and incredible—from the beginning of the twentieth century until the Pacific war. At least, that's the only way I can begin to understand the folly of Japan's policies. But, of course there's another reason. The Japanese are essentially diehard and incredible in the sense that they always do everything most meticulously right to end of what they've undertaken, for better or for worse. They have a "mania for the perfect in their 'cultural DNA': *an incredible and real obsession-cum-complex of always becoming "Number One" in all they undertake*! And this aspect of their character diffused the very special hundred years of Japanese history we're now getting to know a little better. Actually we should extend the dates to, say, roughly between 1850-1883 up until 1950-1955 with the continuation until the present day being purely the economic and commercial side, without big changes in the underlying Japanese mentality.

The collapse of their greed towards "their" New World and their 1945 military capitulation triggered American tutelage and quasi-forced membership of the Western Bloc. And, as far as we are concerned in our philosophical quest, it is in this same context—the proof of failure of "total militiarism"—that a phenomenal "changeover" was also engendered for Aikido.

Aikido today is a consequence of the historical instruments (militarism, expansionist politics, colonialism, economy, societal culture, community phenomena, etc.)) and facts I just mentioned. It is the result of pre-war, ultra-nationalist, paramilitary and extraterritorial Japanese folly and delusions, as exemplified by the invasion and plunder of Manchuria.

Indeed, let's not forget that Morihei Ueshiba taught his art to an elite, above all a political elite and, more precisely, a military elite from the large academies. In that, he was directly implicated in the causes, the means and ideologies of the war*. In short—and not to expand here—his activities, overly close to the corridors of martial and Imperial power, made him a direct actor. It must also be remembered that, since the Meiji era, subordinate only to the Emperor, it was the military caste—even over and above the politicians— which then had the official and legal power in Japan. And this verticality without any counter-power was even written in stone into the 1889 Japanese constitution!

"There is no question but that Aikido was an integral part of the military culture of the time. Nor was there any conflict felt between Omoto's peace-loving New-Heaven-and-New-Earth message and the military culture. Thomas Nadolski [historian] has shown that Omoto had far closer links with ultranationalism than O Sensei's discourses might suggest [at this time because it wasn't the case before the rise of the pre-war Japanese military regime].. " (Thomas Nadolski's doctoral thesis about Omoto: Peter Goldsbury, Aikiweb - Transmission, Inheritance, Emulation # 6 – Wartime Activities of O Sensei and his Students)

So, what about the older Ueshiba—the man of many guises—well, truth is he was quite tainted by the war. The war, for sure, but the war ...? One might ask, what's war? In your opinion, what do you think he actually taught in those elite military academies? Certainly not super-knitting with his wooden sticks. And definitely not the Aikido of love that we talk about today. Rather he taught in a practical way—the 1933 and 1938 Budo-renshu manual of techniques is proof—the most lethal version of the old Daito-ryu Aiki-jujutsu and the use of the weapons he knew so well. That is to say—if we can just bring ourselves to state things crudely here—that he taught what very effectively serves to... kill very effectively.

But teaching to kill effectively is one thing, rather like playing a war game on a video screen or remotely controlling a drone. But to go there, to do it, to see it done, to have to do it, to want to do it, or to have to be there—as most of his academy pupils and mobilized deshi were—that's quite another thing. And I believe that's exactly where the **Gordion-knot aspect of the semantic taboo** within the creation of our Aikido philosophy takes its place in the overall scheme of things.

1942 - I have long believed that Kisshomaru Ueshiba and his father had wanted to "get rid" of or take down—stone by stone, as for a wall—Takeda Sokaku's Daito-ryu. And this, for various reasons related to the art itself, or related to their personalities, or related to their interrelationships.

I also thought for a long time the Americans—because of their post-war ban on it—had more or less forced traditional Japanese martial arts to change. But I now think it didn't happen exactly like that.

First, starting in 1942*, the Americans sought to create files on Japanese who had a direct connection with the corridors of power in the terrifying Japanese war machine. This American service—inter-ally in name only—was called the Supreme Commander for the Allied Powers or, for short, SCAP. That is to say, this group gave priority to targeting the elite military networks, their political and social collaborators, subordinates, collaborators and affiliates. O Sensei would definitely not have been on the front line in this area of research and surveys, but he must certainly have appeared on some lists because of his activities in the various military academies. There he was a teacher of martial arts, instructing in the use of bayonets, knives, bludgeons and throttling devices, arm breakers, swords that pierce and cut, and the like, you know...?

* *"It is interesting that Hans Baerwald was involved in drafting purge criteria for the Dai Nippon Butokukai, which **included Aikido from 1942 onwards**. SCAPINs were directives from SCAP, and the categories listed in SCAPIN 550 need to be read in conjunction with SCAPIN 548, which* *added the Dai Nippon Butokukai, with all its affiliated organizations, to the list of organizations proscribed by SCAP." Extract from "The Occupation of Japan as an Exercise in 'Regime Change' from Hans Baerwald: Reflections after Fifty Years by a Participant", JPRI (Japanese Institute for Political Research) Occasional Papers 29, page 3. Quoted by Peter Goldsbury, Aikiweb, Transmission-Inheritance-Emulation # 06, I: The General Impact of the Pacific War (World War II) on Aikido.*

Thus, for Ueshiba, continuing his "teaching to kill efficiently" gradually became impossible. It seems to me that, above all, it doubtless became irreconcilable with his own cosmic philosophy, the unification of "spirits" side of Omoto (not that of its hard nationalist political right). And, not only his cosmic philosopy, but also his ethics, his own ideas and reflections on life, on the world, and on Aiki itself. And that certainly would be to his credit.

Effectively, without dwelling here on a war turning to vinegar for the Japanese military, at some place in Morihei Ueshiba's honour, there was probably a kind of disgust at what was happening with the war around him. And not only that, but also at his participation along with what was created—his fame—in these elite military and political circles.

In my own considered opinion, it was Morihei Ueshiba's activities—not only in the pre-war extremist military academies since the thirties, but also in the middle of the war at least up until 1942—that eventually lead to the **technical shift in the art**. It was no longer possible for them, father and son (Kisshomaru), to teach their art as is, except by changing its vocation. *Apparently the same problem didn't arise for Takeda Sokaku, who was not—primo—*

yet living in Tokyo and—secundo—not, it seems, involved with the political power of the total-war ultra networks. And—tercio—was not even remotely affected by the rather messy influence of the Omoto religion.

Once we are aware of Morihei Uesiba's predicament, setting aside the actual risk of the Tokyo bombings, I think that we can better understand his retreat to Iwama. Of course, not being a "fly on the wall" of his mind, we cannot really know whether it was aversion to war, remorse for the past, or the fact the war was going badly and, at the same time, fear of being on a SCAP blacklist.

Meanwhile, Kisshomaru Ueshiba, was appointed as the Tokyo organizer responsible for the continuation—for the moment at least—of his father's art *

*Certainly, O Sensei was a bit older (59) when he went to live in Iwama, but why would he leave Kisshomaru in Tokyo if the risk of bombing had been so bad? Who would leave his son in the theater of operations while slipping away to the countryside to grow cabbages and carrots? So there was "something else". Peter Goldsbury gives us part of the answer: "(It) became clear to me that Morihei Ueshiba's own attitude to Aikido organizations was highly ambivalent. On the one hand, he was persuaded of the necessity for them to develop his art; on the other hand, the official version of his life at this time, places more emphasis on his attention to more 'elevated' matters than the mundane affairs of organizations. In addition, the official version also holds that he was really absorbed in his own training regimen and was never really an 'organization' man. As he became increasingly famous and attracted more and more students, he remained relatively disinterested and, therefore—up to a point— 'uncontaminated' by martial art 'politics'. And he left such 'messy' involvement to his son Kisshomaru" (Peter Goldsbury, Transmission-Inheritance-

Emulation, #28, PART ONE – Aikido and Organizations - I: 前菜 / Zensai: Aikido History and Historicism).

We can now better appreciate just where today's Aikido and even its political and social organizations come from. And, above all, we can understand the roots of its fundamental paradox*, namely its taboo, its unspken question of why, for example, were its "dangerous" movements omitted. In fact, the omitted or suppressed movements were the total war movements—shades of Clausewitz—the "difficult" movements and, of course, the secret movements, above all.

The Uneducated in power: While Aikido softened in its general technique compared to that of the "terrifying" brutality of ancient Daito-ryu and also, since it was too terribly effective, in relation to its pre-war martial education, it is reproached today for its apparent lack of efficiency. What a turnaround, what a theatrical twist!

In this way, "lunacy or folly" in one observer's opinion is often a "stroke of genius" in that of another, *and it's here that the notion of a tool's **"vocation"** comes into the picture.* All the explanation I've just given about Aikido's philosophy, its peculiarity above all to be the opposite of a Platonism, its concept of concordance and non-competition, and so on, only makes sense if we believe one thing. Namely that Aikido, in and of itself, had—and has today—eliminated, erased, or at least largely reconsidered the errors of its youth when it was deemed to be "the king of the world" and a "universal panacea". This would be the last tautological "epitaph" of Aikido's militarist ideology.*

* *While one cannot agree with him on certain points, good reference documents on this subject are the well-informed interviews of Elis Amdur*

and his book entitled Dueling with O-Sensei: Grappling with the Myth of the Sage Warrior, specifically Chapter nine, "Tenchi: Head in the Clouds and Feet in the Muck".

In fact, we understand this even better after Kisshomaru Ueshiba's capitulation or concession: Aikido wasn't deemed to be king of the world for good reasons. Must we then revive the old Japanese martial arts concept—also found in the former Daito-ryu and elsewhere—and so go from the sabre of death to the sword of life* ... ?

* *The sword of life* 活人剣 *(Katsujinken). Akira Kurosawa and the fundamental theme of his film "The Seven Samurai" (*活人剣*:* **Katsujinken,** *the sword that preserve life and its oposite,* 殺人剣, **Satsujinken,** *the sword that destroye life.*

Now it was there—in this sabre of death—that the taboo of Aikido—the burdensome "unsaid" in its heavy heart—is entrenched. It's there that the "prohibition" in contemporary Aikido stands—a prohibition, a taboo, which must not be thought of, not to be discussed, mentioned or even alluded to.

And this taboo is a great pity because, in fact, this story of Aikido has made a commendable shift and, for the moment, continues on in a rather beautiful and honourable way.

AIKIDO'S GORDIAN KNOT MOMENT

- At this point, I would like to bring to the reader's mind the words of the theoretical physicist J. Robert Oppenheimer, design manager at Los Alamos and known as "the father of the atomic bomb". After it was dropped, he quoted from the Hindu script Bhagavad-Gita and said, "Now I am become Death, the destroyer of worlds".

These sentiments—sentiments which help us understand the shift in Aikido—were echoed by the physicist Albert Einstein. He co-signed a letter to the U.S. president, urging the creation of an "atomic bomb" but later had profound regrets about his act and said, "War cannot be humanized, it can only be abolished".

The Gordion knot moment within the formation process of Aikido and also within today's Aikido—the prohibition or taboo on talking about its warlike origins (such as *the Minamoto no Yoshimitsu brothers' eleventh-century macabre researches, one of Aiki's great foundations*) was engendered by "**The War**". Because war is—in and of itself—a pure trauma, a horror—except, of course, for those who stay home and profit from it.

And so, as always and like everywhere in the world, the taboo concerns exactly all that war involves or has involved. In other words, loathsome servitude, shameful personal decisions, various wounds, active or passive cowardice, horrors, false joys or pride, degrading manipulation, conniving, collaboration and complicity as well as catastrophic illusions. But also true disgust, true shame, even ignominy, execration, filth, and finally disaster and trauma for belligerents on both sides.* *In the Asia-Pacific conflict of 1937-1945,* ***several tens of millions*** *dead or missing on both sides, with China having the heaviest tally.*

One could talk about the war experiences of Yamaguchi Sensei (submariner, kamikaze pilot), Okumura Sensei, Tomiki Sensei (who ended the war as a prisoner in a Russian camp), and many other Ueshiba alumni. Above all, one could especially talk here about Shirata Rinjiro, one of Ueshiba Morihei's most fabulous and close pre-war uchi-deshi who stopped Aikido for almost twenty years after his return from war. Nobody will ever know just what he had to do over there, and it is probably better that way. In any event, in a highly symbolic gesture, he sealed the blade of one of his Katana (sword) in its scabbard in a durable way so that no one or even him, could never use it again ... (It's twenty years later and on the insistence and without any doubt or explanations about Morihei's and Kisshomaru's focus on "The New Aikido" that he "resumed service" in the teaching of what would eventually become the Aikido of peace and harmony ... modern Aikido).

In fact, it suddenly became necessary to make a significant shift in meaning of the sabre of death (Koroshiai). The militarist sabre and the "ideology of assassination" of 1930s Japan had collapsed on the momentous occasion of unconditional Japanese surrender. And with it, "war"—as a value of power, power to win at the cost of lives—suddenly became worthless and had to be redirected towards something more viable, more vital, more ... downright "clean".

And so the shift—in reality a U-turn—was towards the second "slope" of Aiki (each mountain has two different sides, another very traditional Japanese notion), in other words, towards "a sabre of life". (Ikinokori version of Katsujinken: the sabre that gives life*, the protector sabre and, above all, ironically the protector of war itself.

** **Ikinokori/Koroshiai**. Let's revisit these two very important concepts so as to understand this almost natural shift from an Aikid of war to an Aiki of peace; two typical and parallel concepts of ancient Japanese martial arts.*

*« **Katsujinken** (活人剣): live-giving sword. Sen no sen = initiate the attack by grabbing the opponent and throwing him. Sen sen is to attack first and overcome. This is winning with Kiai.*

***Setsujinken** (切人剣): death-dealing sword. Go no sen = first evade an opponent's attack, then strike and control him, to eventually finish him off.*

(Explanations taken from: Stanley A. Pranin, Aiki News # 88 - Interview with Tokimune Takeda - 1991. See also in the Aiki news article: "Satsujinken and Katsujinken" by Dane S. Harden)

To put it more succinctly, it was imperative that—at this point in time—the Aiki tool change… its vocation*!

* I assiduously kept close to Sasaki Masando Sensei (see my translation of his very interesting last three months of classes at the Tokyo Aikikai, in my book: "Secrets of Kokyu-Ho", at Budo-Editions). Masando Sensei was himself also a direct, albeit late and almost anachronistic, product of the nationalist and ethnocentric currents of the "ultra" Japan. And I can allow myself to say here that the cracked, fissured varnish completely hides an interesting depth in so far as a reflection is concerned. So stopping at the imperialist or political varnish of History—its almost immersive context for the Japanese of that era, Ueshiba Morihei included—doesn't allow one to fathom its results with lucidity. After all, political or moral emotion is here the enemy of the philosopher. On the other hand, if all this is still taboo in today's Japan, it shows that the embers are not yet extinguished. One can have niggling doubts about whether these "errors" of former times have been completely digested or thought over in the political circles (among the hawks still in power), in high society, or even in Japanese Aikido. Worlds can rapidly change, even in the blink of any eye—collapse, rise up, do an about turn or stand up, explode, and dissolve—but the deep cultures and the typical human mentalities change much less quickly.

Let us quote Peter Goldsbury here: "Another interpretation, however, might focus more on two aspects of the transformation that Kisshomaru doesn't emphasize. First, a local dojo [Kobukan] became a special type of organization. And, secondly, the reason behind this was that, following its 'elevation' [to an official rank recorded by the Japanese military administration of the time (thirties and forties)], the organization [Ueshiba's Kobukai] became a more appropriate instrument for waging the war more efficiently. This is why the government reformed the Dai Nippon Butokukai in 1942 and also why Aikido was given its official name and taken under the wing of this reformed organization on the same date. Ouch, >that's it, maybe we've the answer to the question of why 1942! It was shortly after the reform of the organization [Kobukai] that Morihei Ueshiba moved to Iwama.

One interpretation of the move to Iwama is that Ueshiba was fundamentally peace-loving. On this point, opinions diverge, for example, those of Peter Goldsbury and E. Admur. For my part, however, the text of the interview I translated above suggests to me that Moriheai Ueshiba lived a little "on another planet". I sincerely believe that, at a given moment in time—possibly during or just after 1942—he had transcended the idea of war, of rivalry, of competition. And this, not only technically, but also intellectually. It's worthwhile remembering that the naval Battle of Midway—with its attendant losses and huge uproar in Japan—took place in June 42. Suddenly "to be peaceful" or "not to be peaceful was no longer as important as one thought:

Ueshiba had risen above all that. And I admit that's a little disturbing. But let's continue with Peter's text]: One interpretation of the Iwama move is that a fundamentally peace-loving Ueshiba became equally fundamentally disenchanted with the bellicose aims and methods of the Japanese military elite he had associated with for the previous twenty years. An English term for this is 'metanoia.' It is a term that has been anglicized from its orinal Greek and means a complete change in one's thinking or way of life (resulting from penitence or a spiritual conversion)" (Peter Goldsbury, in Aikiweb, Transmission-Inheritance-Emulation #28 (part one), II: 吸い物 / Suimono: Establishment of the Kobukai/ IAF).

So, having digressed to explore these important observations, I come back to my final conclusion. Following the 1942-1955 shift, through the practice of contemporary Aikido, today there is finally a philosophy which aims at putting forward this "Aikido jewel" in the martial arts crown. Or, as some of its partisans see it, this pure diamond magnificently extracted from its worthless, black gangue.

Nonetheless, it has to be said that its current epithets—sweetness, radiance, bloom, flamboyance, "love", dynamism and magnificence—often hide, rather badly, its philosophical reality. But the philosophy is there: it's a philosophy dictated by events, of congruence with the world. It's a philosophy that targets—through its practice (praxis)—experiential convergences as well as establishment of the "you" (but also of me, you, him, us, them) as the subject of what's happening. In other words, it's a refocusing of the individual being. And this, through an absolutely ontological and global (holistic) perspective of intimate union "with the worlds". What we can even call now an ethic, but, above all, not a morality.

So, if I may be permitted an internet metaphor, we are surfing here between a classical (ancient) metaphysics and a modern phenomenology. I say metaphysics because this mixture of empiricism—knowledge flows from my experience—and idealism—I am the subject of what I think—has a direct correspondance with what we experience over years of training in Aikido. And, as for modern phenomenology, because this philosophical study of the structures of experience and consciousness, almost always—at one moment or another—opens out into the substance of the art itself and the life of its actor, that is to say on the research of the lived "essences".

Yes, phenomenology for sure but, since the subject of Japan itself largely lies outside—eludes, if you prefer—all Western categories, I am not sure if, as in university phenomenology, one can talk about "sciences of essences". But in any case, this is what I often feel during my wanderings in the world of Aikido. I might add that the Do here is, for me, strictly a limitative framework for the practice, allowing control of its course and limits in a paternalistic manner. The Do being the disciplinary and normative axis of martial arts: "Atten..shun! Answer all present! At ease!

The phenomenology of "love" and or peace is interesting because it has two facets or aspects: one practical—physical training—and the other intellectual, the questioning of essences. Moreover, one of them doesn't work without the other, which is surprisingly similar to many traditional ancient philosophies. In this way, its setting in a presentation of modernity introduces a point of particular interest that says: "Peace, love, is what you will do with it". Or, perhaps one can put it better by saying, "You will do a wonderful job in Aikido if you yourself become a wonderful being". Phew, it's not over yet!

In bringing it closer to structuralism this time, in this respect—in the absence of being systemic—one could, for a number of reasons, speak at this point of a systemic philosophy.

Firstly, the philosophy of Aikido—though a system in and of itself—works nicely for a family of systems and, as such, is a very special and real organisation called a hyperonym. In this respect, Aikido can be studied in its own right.

Secondly, its relationship with history, or "the histories of the different eras", clearly shows—at the risk of making it an "orphan"—its true nature, its dependence on these systems.

And, finally, it is this "haystack-like" assembly—with Aikido in the rôle of the "needle"—which serves as the philosophy of Aikido. Truth is that, if this assembly were to be dissassembled, then Aikido would loose its coherence. And this is, in fact, its current risk. After all we have seen on the long road of its history and all that has been revealed about the seemingly dichotomous past of the art of Aikido, this must indeed be its greatest paradox.

CONCLUSION - We have seen how—although the reasoning has certainly been over concise here—one can start start to define a real and up-to-date Aikido philosophy. And it's important to understand that finally mature—this time, at long last removed from the matrix of history—it can become timeless. And it is this that makes for its new power and, at the same time, its new legitimacy.

So, we must confine to the dustbin of history Aikido genres that are "populist", "sporting", modern, traditional, technical, historical, militaristic, and moralizing. And, along with them, those that are deem themselves superior, genre Western Christian-Platonic theory of "competition versus forgiveness" and Japanese militarist theory of Budo being the only mode of universal excellence.

Then, faced with the extraordinarily powerful Aikido philosophy that emerges—*how many practical philosophies of peace and pacifism do you know that work as well as Aikido*—we must also set aside Morihei Ueshiba's almost imcomprehensible "mythical, mystical, Shintoistic, and Omoto" Aikido. Yes, even Morihei Ueshiba's Aikido since, while truly congenial for sure, within the context of our modernity, it can only be put into practice with difficulty—except as a key to understanding the slow construction of Aikido.

All dissonances between antinomic, dual, or humanly overclassified perspectives effectively become purely "subsidiary" components of a system of "intimate concordance".

Because now, it is developments of "**this creative power without rivalry—springing from a constellation concordant with all world of events** — which can little by little reconcile practitioners, leaders and authorities in a unified Aikido. And an Aikido that is finally… its very own conqueror.

And if these words give rise to some fear or are, in some way, discouraging, this concept, this "soul" of Aikido can also be described in the same way as in its history since its Taoistic beginnings. Namely, "the tilting of competition and duality towards the "One" of In and Yo, whose addition is always equal to... zero*!"

* *Recall: Zero—the emptiness or vacuum—is like the essential keystone of the ciphering of Aikido and of its "cosmic" coding: five bodies to reunite in my action of life; times two—tori plus uke—or more: like many uke in training. Because it's here we find here our original "mu" (無 or 无)—meaning no thing—so fundamental in Aikido, for example, in the expression Mu-Ken ("without sword" 無), Mugamae ("without guard" 無構), Muyoku ("without lust" 無欲), Mushin ("without desire" 無心), and Mufu ("Calm" (無風).*

These terms must surely remind the reader of something? Of course, it is **to be well oriented** (or well placed), **to have confidence, to be considerate,** and finally, **to cooperate.**

Thank you for your patience, Peace and wisdom be with you.

EXTRACT

Excerpt from an interview with Morihei Ueshiba, 1957 in the book *Aikido* published by Kisshomaru Ueshiba, at Kôwa (page 219) in the original version of the Japanese edition.

問B　合気は武の道であると共に神の教えでもあるわけですね。そこで合気道の精神は……。

植芝　合気とは「愛」であり、天地の大愛を心として、あらゆるものを愛護することを自己の使命としなければならない。その使命を完遂するのが真の武の道でなければならない。真の武は自己に打克ち、敵の戦う心をなくす……いや、敵そのものをなくしてしまう絶対的な自己完成への道なのです。そして合気の武技は天の理法を体得して、霊肉一体の至上境にまで到達するまでの業であり道程なのです。

問B　合気は世界平和への道ということになりますね。

植芝　地上天国の出現こそ究極の目的です。ともかく、世界中が和合しなければならない。そうすれば原爆も水爆も、その必要がなくなって、住みよい、楽しい世界になりますよ。

---+---

That's it.
Thank you for your attention.
I hope this all-too-short summary of Aikido, its history and its basic philosophy, will have allowed you to clarify your approach to this ancestral and profound art.

Through this essay, I would like to thank my past and present masters, and all those who, over the decades, have enriched my research and knowledge, and allowed me to write this essay.

Olivier GAURIN - Tokyo, Japan - July, 2018

--- + ---

END

CREDITS

*- First of all, thank you to the **ATELIER KATSURA** who fundamentally revised the English translation of this book with tenacity and relevance. This translation in English language allows, directly by synergy, to make also French readers benefit from his remarks, corrections, handshakes, syntaxes and rajoches.*

*- Tokyo, the first text's test of "History of Aikido received a first spell check in french in May 2016 by **LUC GIRARDIN**. Big thanks to him.*

*- Thanks to **GUILLAUME ÉRARD** for his faithful friendship, his lighting and his research also on certain points of the text, among others on the Daitô-Ryû;*

*- Thanks to **ÉRIC GROUSILLAT** for the generosity of his research and his tirelessness in these matters of Japanese language and Aikido;*

*- Thanks to **PETER GOLDSBURY** for his admirable and hard work on the historical truth of Aikido in general;*

*- Thanks to **ELIS ADMUR** for its new and critical insights on Aikido, which also benefits this book, and therefore readers;*

*- Thanks to **CHRISTOPHER LI** of Aikido Sangenkai for his interviews, decryptions of Aikido, or decipherings of the history of Aikido.*

*- Thanks to **JOHN STEVENS** for his analyzes and his various research on Aikido which will benefit the readers of this book;*

*- Also thanks to **WILLIAM GLEASON** who always knew how to divulge an Aikido faithful to many of the themes of this book;*

*- A certain thanks to **SEISHIRO ENDO** for his contribution to the central lighting of the philosophy of Aikido which benefits this book, and therefore the reader;*

*- A big thank finally, and posthumous, to **STANLEY PRALIN**, who through his research work, throughout his life, allowed that practitioners, or researchers like me, can know a little more about their art.*

O.G.